ESSENTIAL GUIDE TO

DRAWING

Still Life

ESSENTIAL GUIDE TO

DRAWING

Still Life

A PRACTICAL AND INSPIRATIONAL WORKBOOK

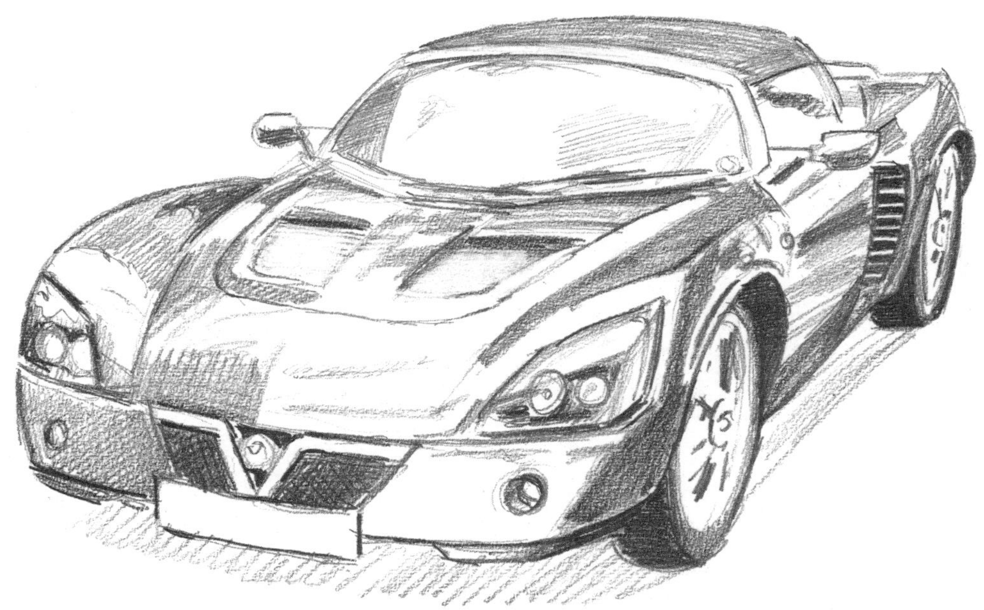

BARRINGTON BARBER

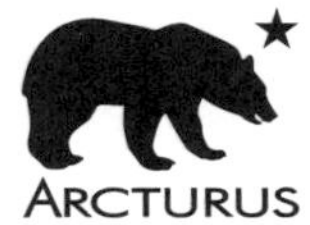

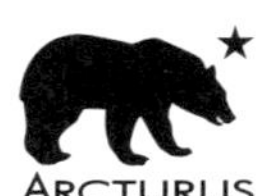

This edition published in 2019 by Arcturus Publishing Limited
26/27 Bickels Yard, 151–153 Bermondsey Street,
London SE1 3HA.

ISBN: 978-1-78888-898-1
AD002352UK

Printed in China

CONTENTS

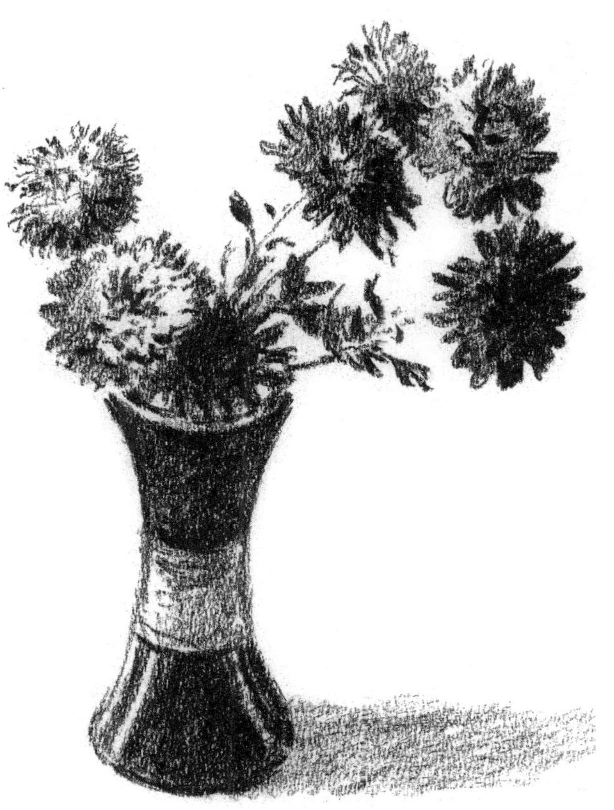

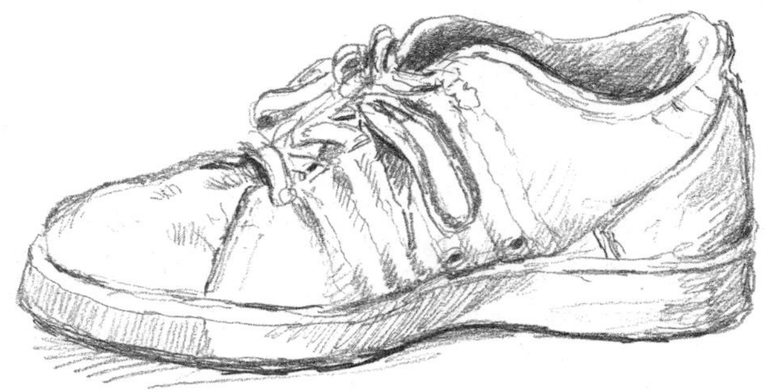

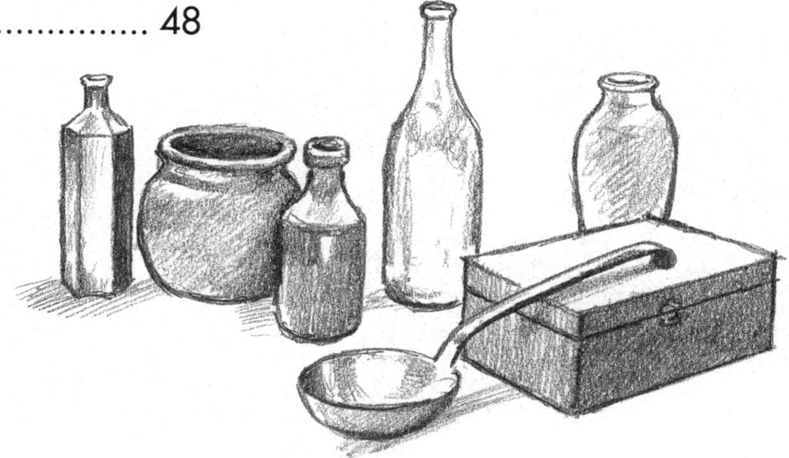

Introduction

As a genre, still life is the most accessible way for artists to practise their skills. Objects of all sorts are always easily available to draw, and even in your own house you will find numerous still-life arrangements that have occurred without any effort on your part. Still life encourages you to look closely before you have even set pencil to paper. Observe how a single object rests upon a surface: what angle will you choose; what texture does it have; are there any highlights or shadows playing upon it? Again, a group of objects makes a different set of demands on your powers of observation, because you are looking at things in relation to one another and considerations of proportion and perspective will come into play. From the exercises in this book you will learn about the ways in which you can build up a pleasing still-life composition and gain some practice in the genre.

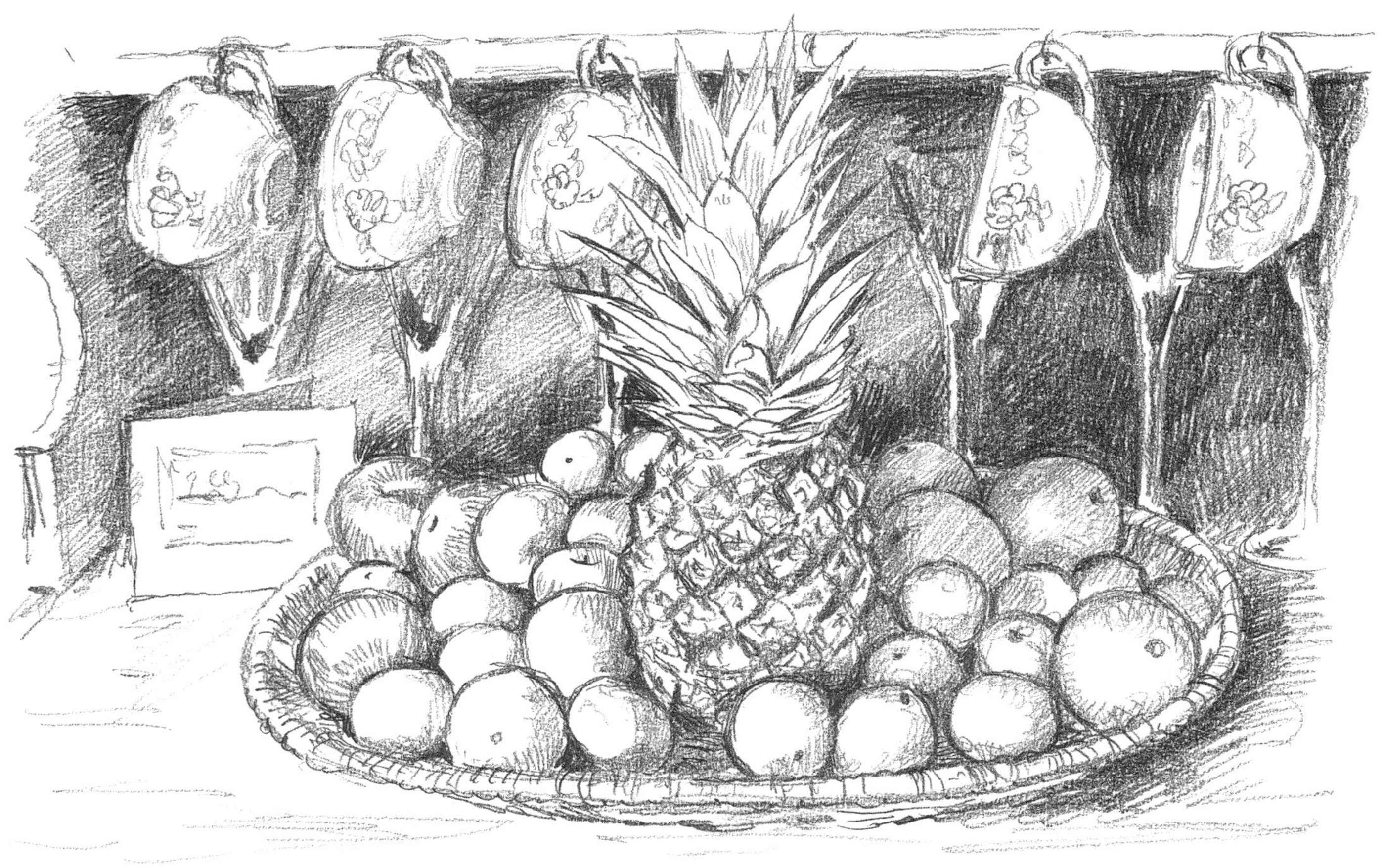

Materials

Any medium is valid for drawing still life and I have shown a range of possibilities here and later in the book. The suitability of the medium you choose depends on what you are trying to achieve. You probably don't need to buy all the items listed below, and it is wise to experiment gradually. Start with the range of pencils suggested, and when you feel you would like to try something different, do so. For paper, I suggest starting with a medium-weight cartridge paper.

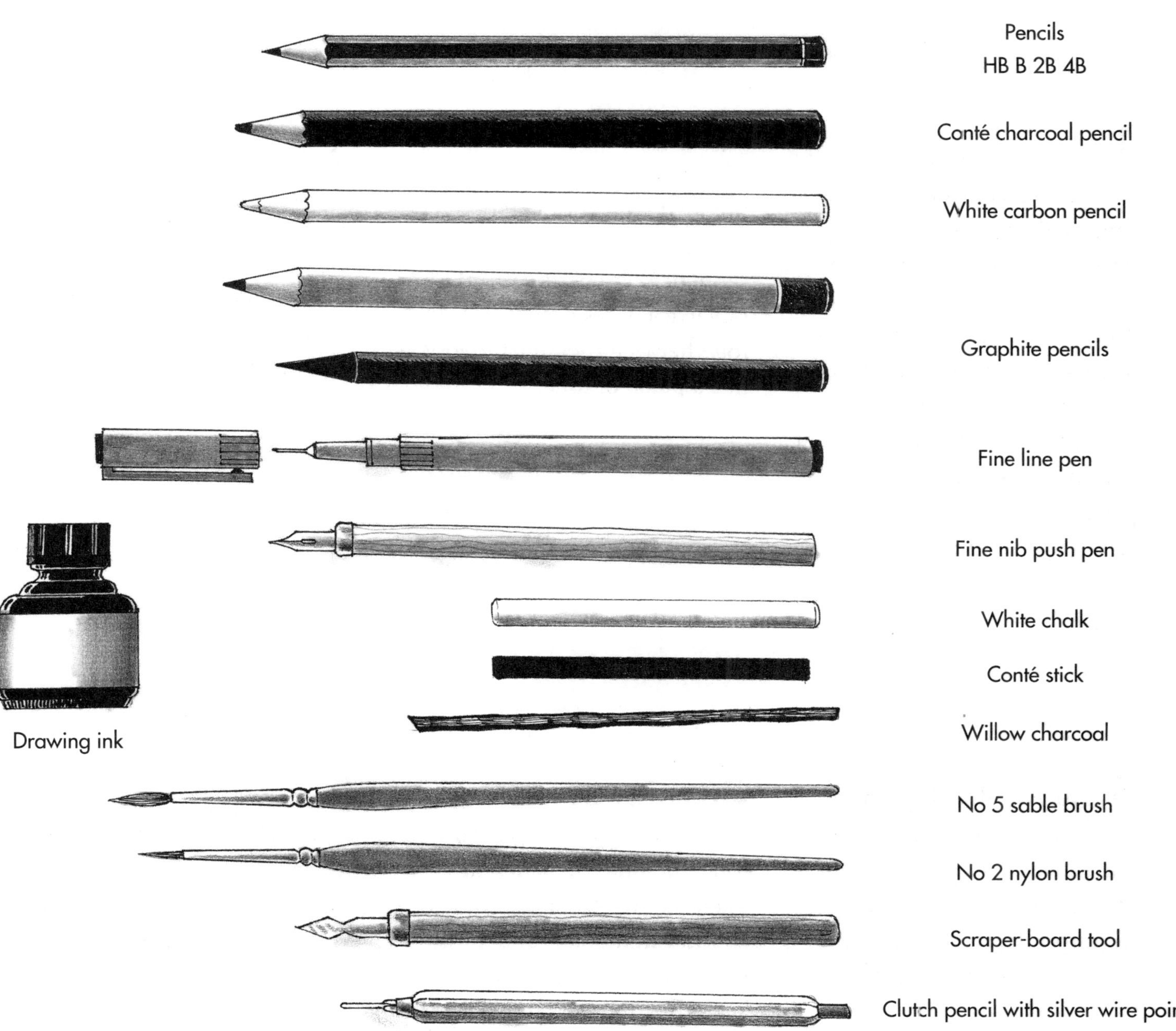

Simple Marks

Before we make a start on drawing objects from the real world, it's a good idea to practise some simple exercises as a warm-up. While these first pages are primarily intended for beginners, you'll find that the exercises are still useful even if you've had a good deal of practice.

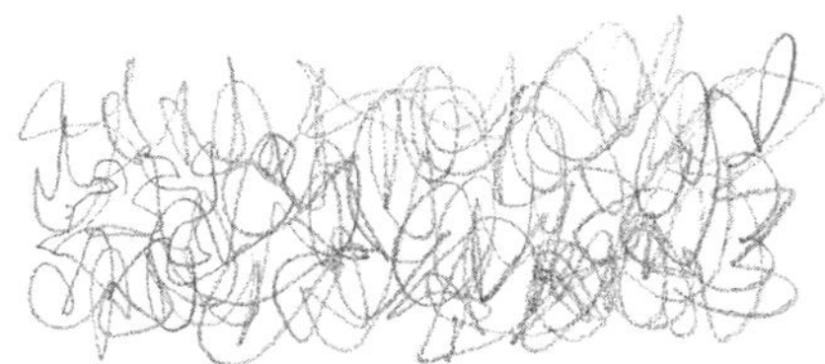

1. To make a start, try drawing a wavering, continuous line that repeatedly overlaps itself. As you draw, note the effect of the pencil on the surface of the paper. This first exercise is really just to encourage you to realize that the feel of your materials is just as important as the visual result. Without this understanding you'll find that your drawing lacks tactile values.

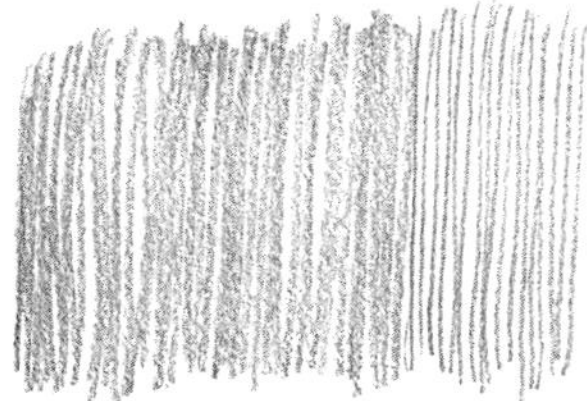

2. When you feel you have pursued your scribble for long enough, try out a simple sequence of repetitive strokes of vertical lines drawn so close together that they start to look like a patch of tone.

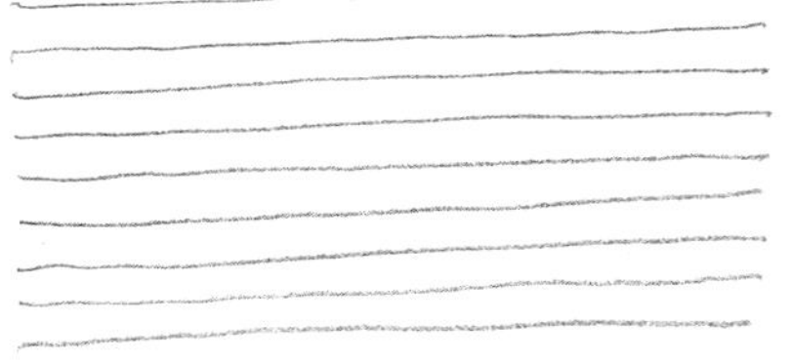

3. Then try some horizontal lines that are more spaced out and are all about the same length, the same distance apart and as straight as you can make them. You are beginning to control your pencil to achieve an effect.

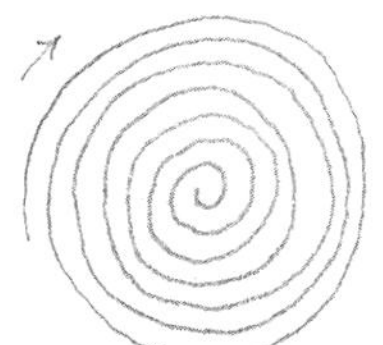

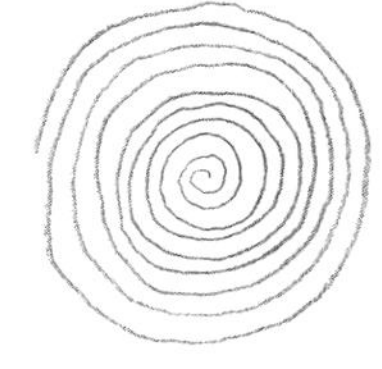

4. Now try drawing a spiral that starts on the outside edge and moves slowly inwards until you reach the centre. Then do the opposite, starting in the centre and spiralling outwards.

5. Next lay down a whole rectangle of medium to dark tone, moving the pencil in diagonal strokes as naturally as you can manage and always in the same direction. Try to keep the tone the same all over.

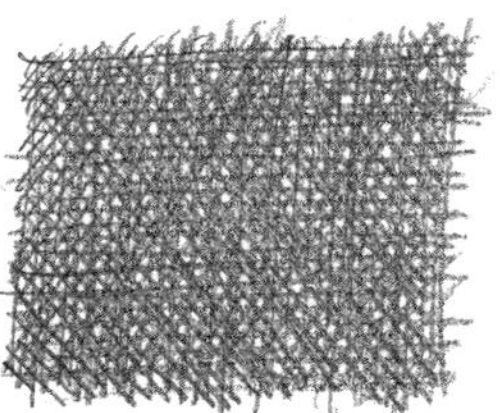

6. Make a layer of vertical strokes close together, followed by a layer of horizontals going across them, then by diagonals crossing in both directions. You'll see this builds up a dark tone.

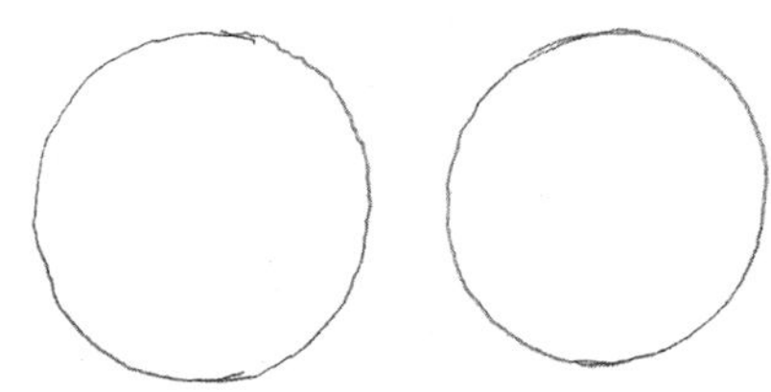

7. Now try drawing a circle as perfectly as you can. Then imagine a perfect circle in your mind and try drawing a circle again. This is not so easy as the previous exercises but is very good practice.

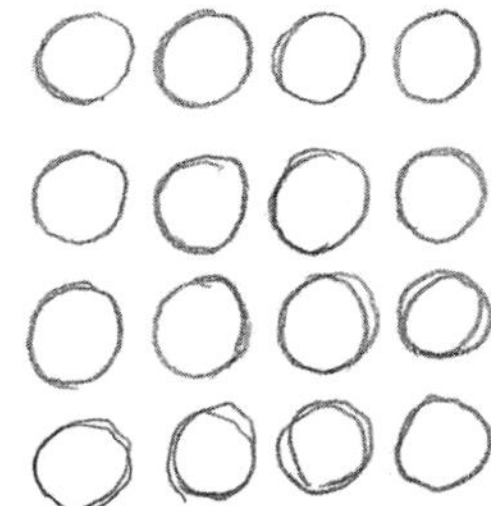

8. Draw several small circles, lining them up in rows of four or five. The idea is to make them as similar as possible and in regular formation. You are now dividing up space and organizing shapes.

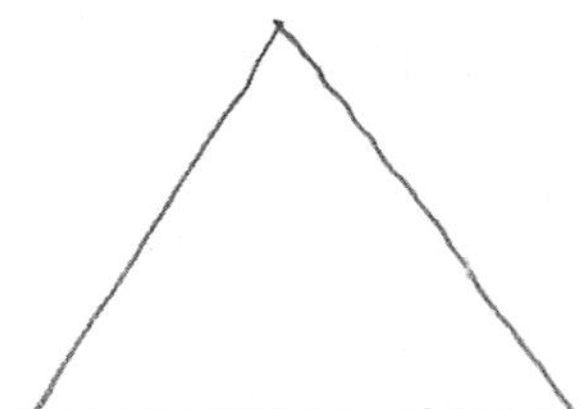

9. Next comes a series of simple conceptual shapes, starting with an equilateral triangle – that is, one with all sides equal.

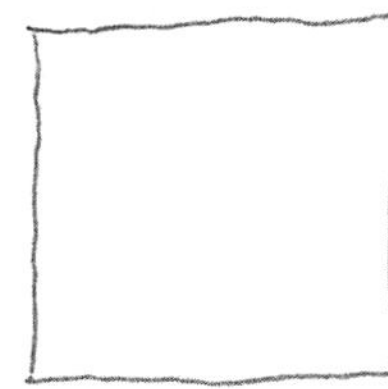

10. Now try a square, remembering that all sides should be the same length and all corners are right angles.

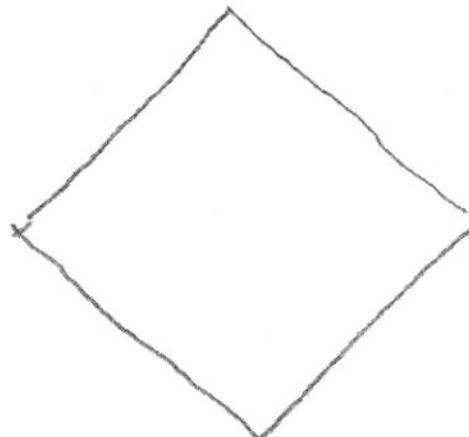

11. Now draw the same shape but tilted up so that it stands on one corner – slightly more tricky to do.

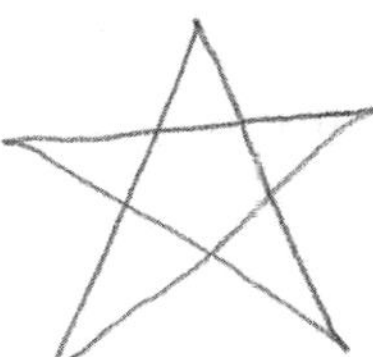

12. Without taking your pencil off the paper, draw a five-pointed star. This may need a few attempts before you get it right.

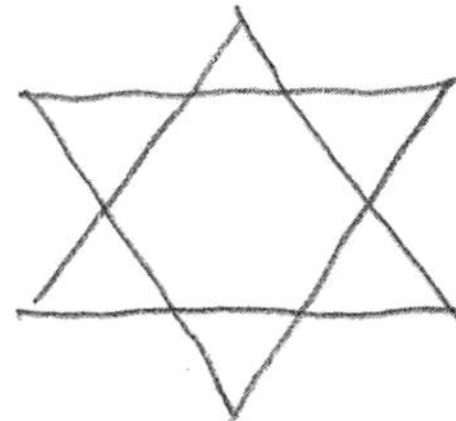

13. Now draw two equilateral triangles overlapping to make a six-pointed star.

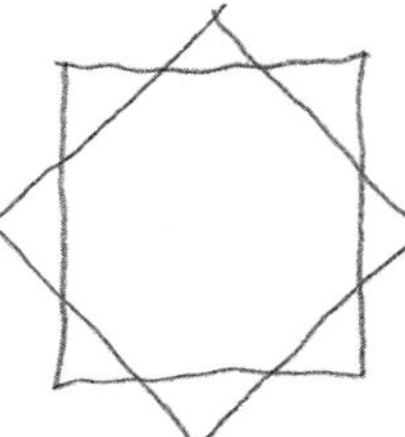

14. And after that, two squares overlapping to make an eight-pointed star.

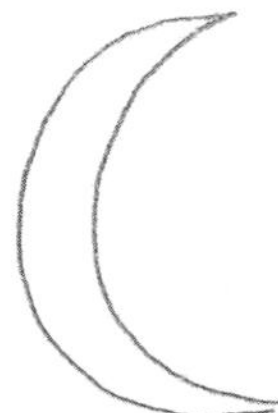

15. Now draw a crescent moon shape, which is parts of two circles overlapping.

Shading Practice

The next step is to concentrate more on tone in order to draw apparently three-dimensional shapes.

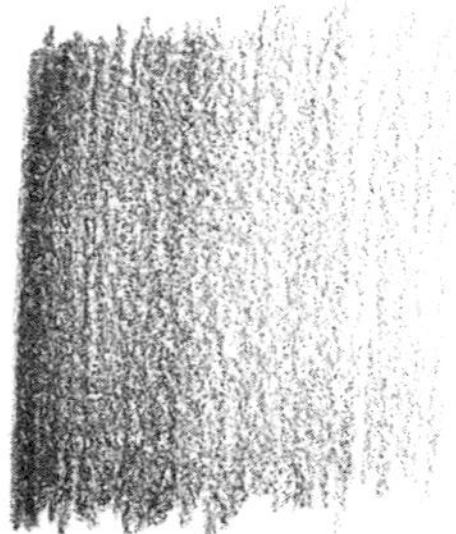

1. To start with, draw some shading, using vertical strokes that gradually get lighter until they disappear altogether.

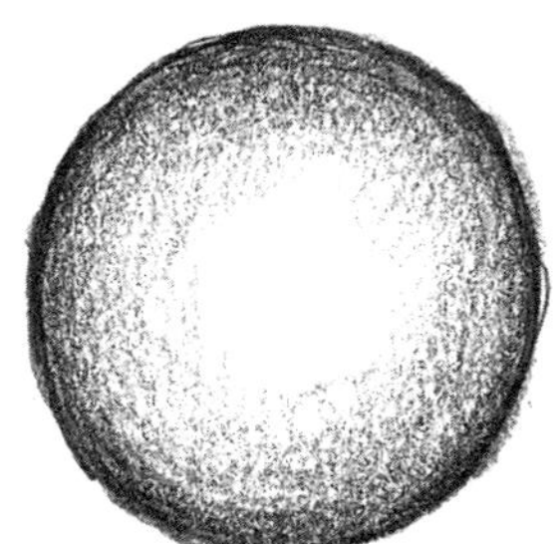

2. Now draw a circle and shade in around the outer rim, making the tone gradually lighter and lighter as you approach the centre. As you can see, this resembles a sphere.

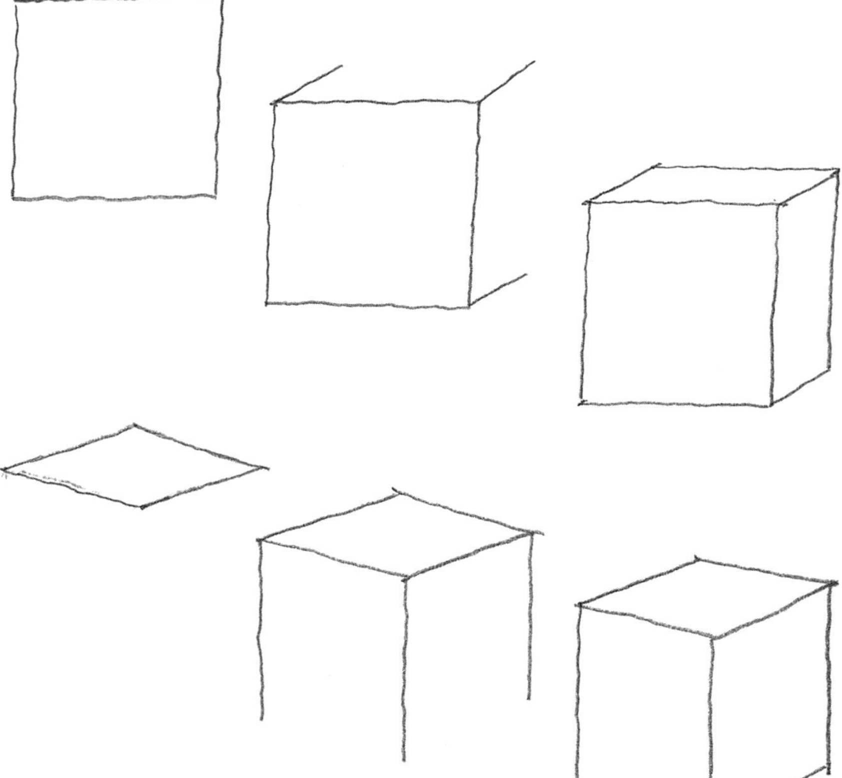

3. Draw a square, then draw three parallel lines from three of the corners, as shown. Draw two more lines parallel to the edge of the square. What appears before your eyes is a conventional representation of a cube shape – a three-dimensional object.

4. A way to do a similar figure is to draw a flattened diamond shape, extend three verticals from the corners and then join their ends to make another cube.

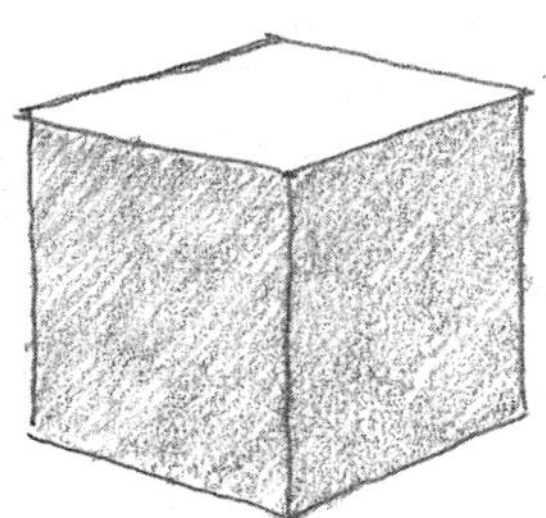

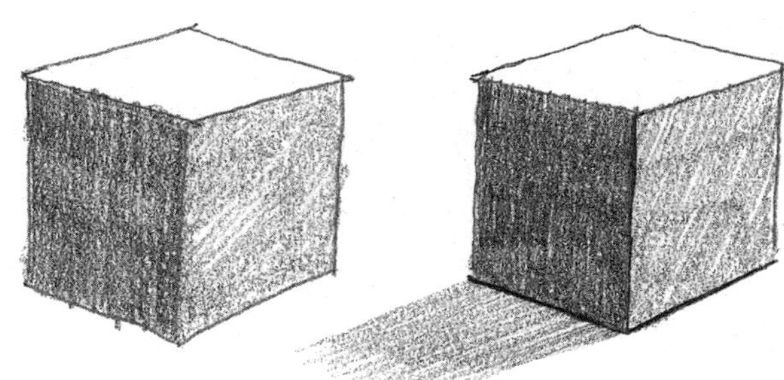

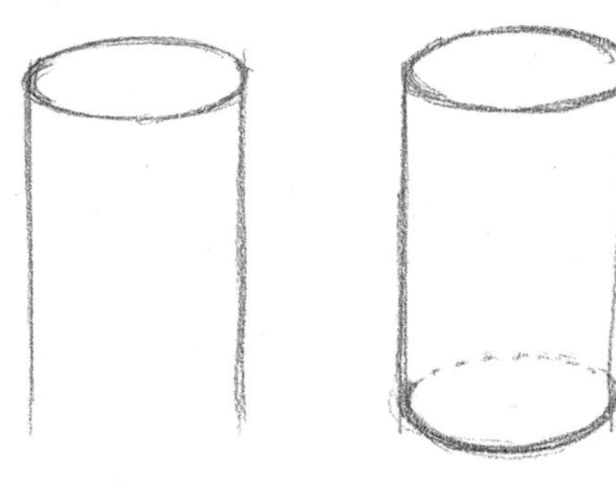

5. Give this last figure a three-dimensional quality by shading in the two lower surfaces of the cube with an even tone – not too dark. Then work over the left-hand surface with a slightly darker tone. Draw in a cast shadow stretching away from the darker side of the cube. All this has the effect of making the cube look even more solid.

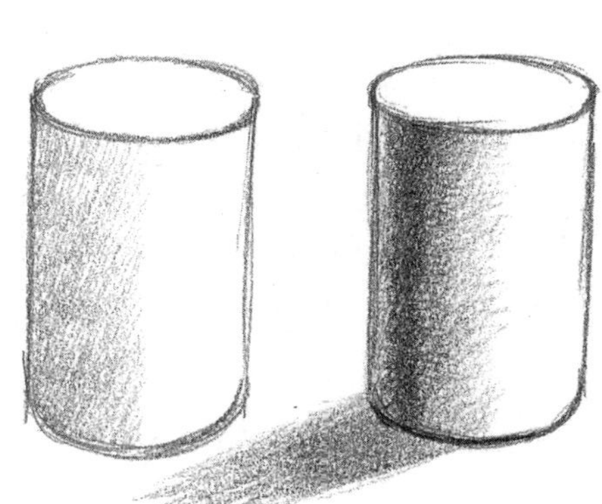

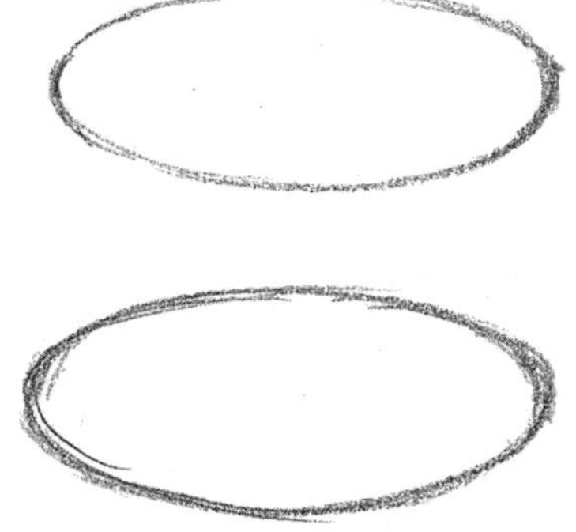

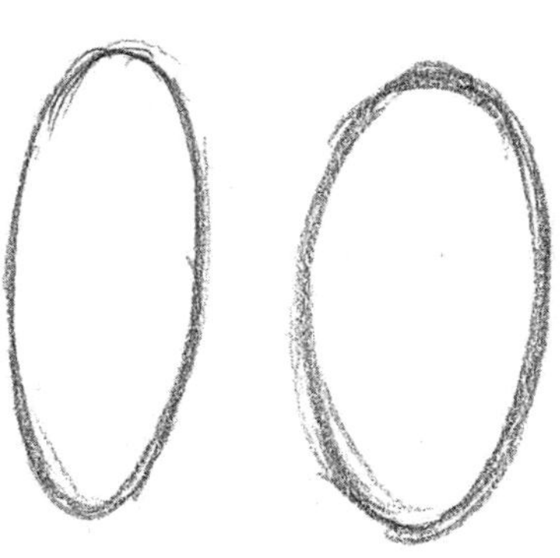

6. The next exercise is to draw some ellipses, which are curved shapes that resemble a circle seen from an oblique angle. If you look at a wine glass, the top edge and the base will appear to be ellipses unless you are viewing it from immediately above. Draw several of these to get the idea, remembering that the curve must be continuous, without any flattened bits or pointed ends. Depict some of them on their narrow ends so that they resemble a wheel seen from an angle.

7. You can now use your ellipse-drawing skill to depict a cylinder. Draw the ellipse, then project two vertical lines downwards from the narrow edges. Draw a second ellipse at the lower end of the two straight lines. To make the cylinder appear solid, rub out the top edge of this ellipse.

When you've done that, shade very lightly down the left-hand side of the cylinder, allowing the tone to fade off to nothing about halfway across the length. Darken a strip down the left-hand side of this shadow, not quite touching the side of the cylinder. Finally, put in a cast shadow as you did with the cube.

Basic Drawing of Single Objects

For your next practice, find a number of ordinary objects from around the house and have a go at drawing them in a simple way. There's no need to look for items with inherent beauty – this is just about learning to draw things accurately.

Find an ordinary wooden box and do your best to reproduce it as I have done here, with its perspective effect. Notice how the far end of the box appears to be slightly smaller than the closer end.

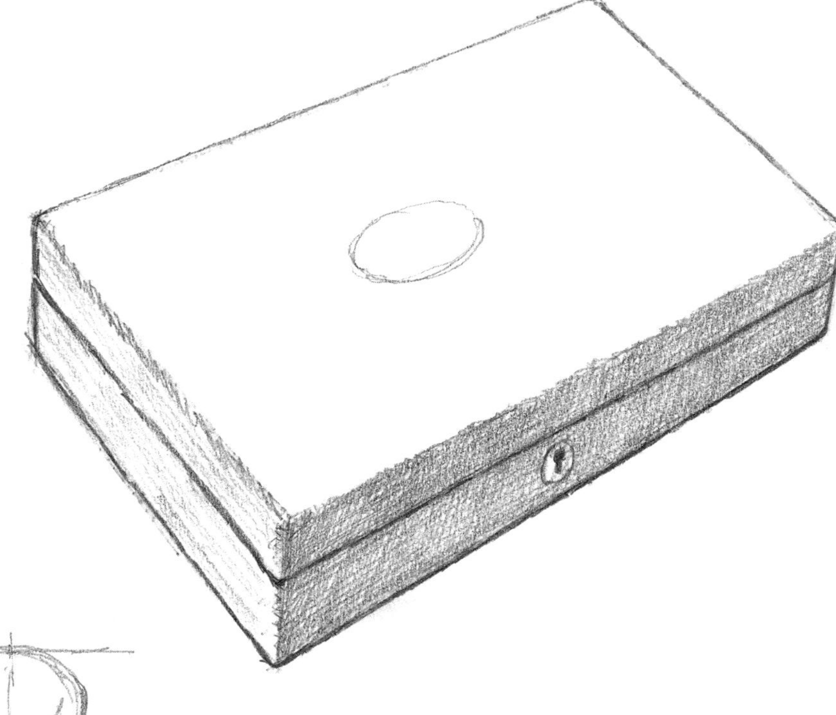

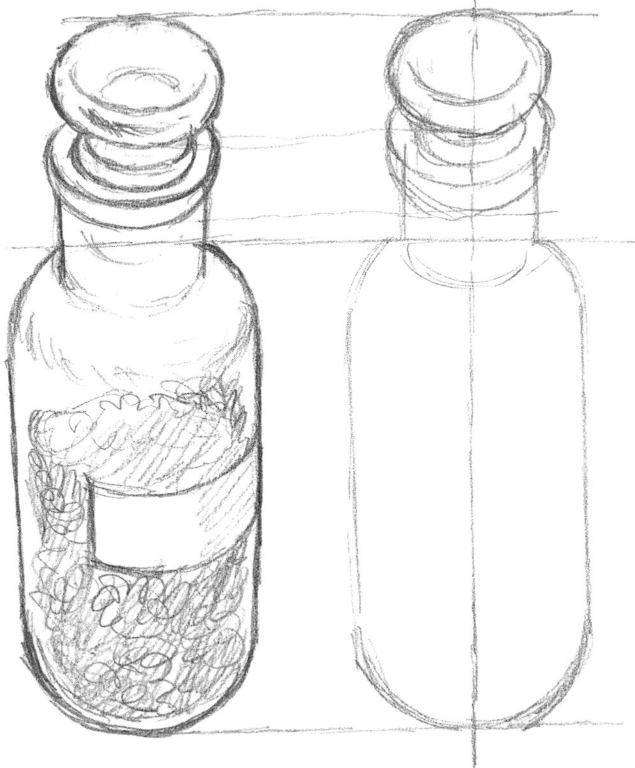

Here's a little glass bottle containing some pigment that I found in my studio. It is based on a circular shape so, as you can see in the drawing next to it, the sides show as mirror images either side of a central line.

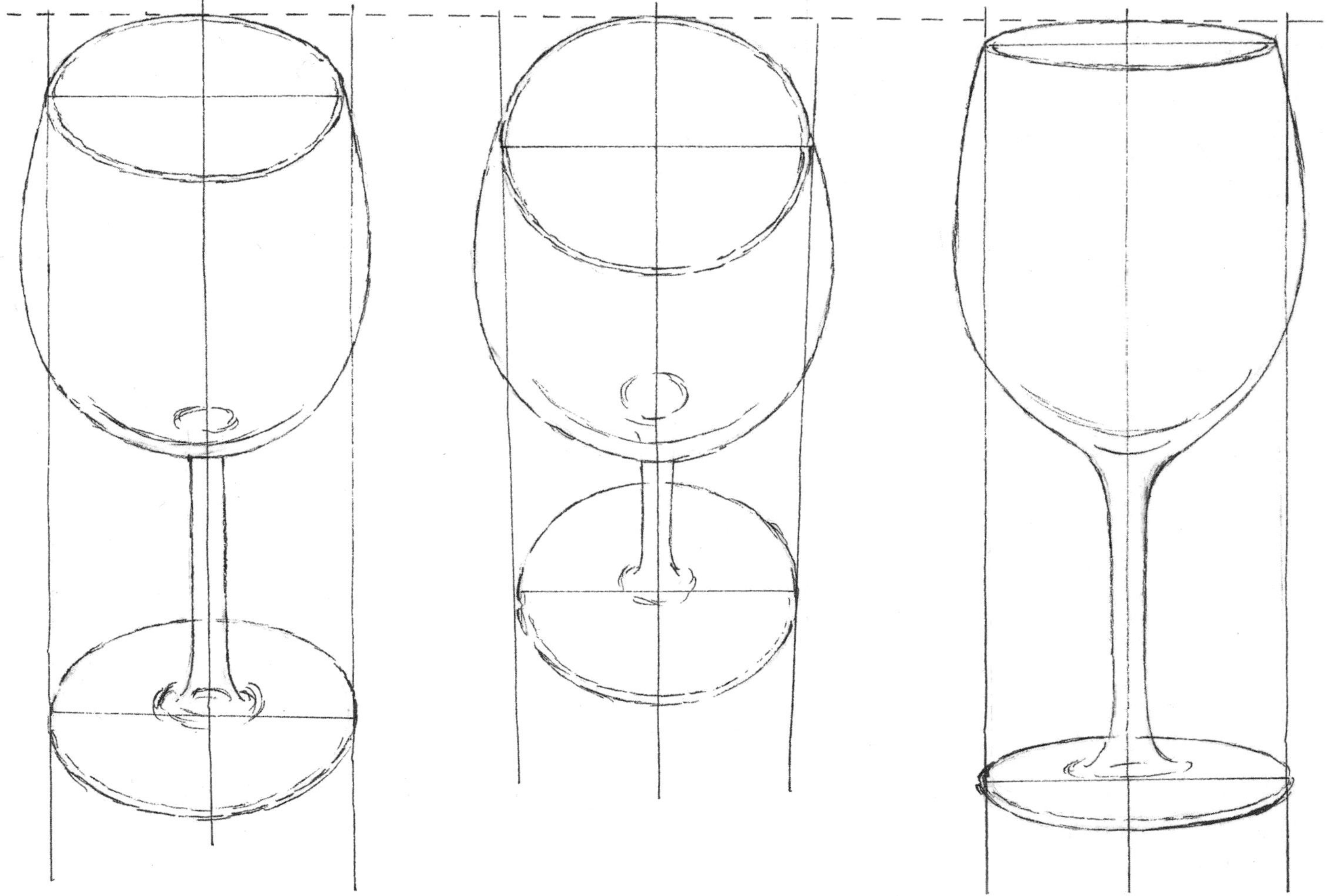

Now find a straightforward object like a wine glass, which has an interesting shape; its transparency enables you to see the structure clearly. Begin by getting some idea of the proportions of the glass; calculate the ratio of stem length to bowl size. As with the glass bottle opposite, draw a vertical ruled line to mark the centre line of the object. The shape of the glass is curved, so the two sides should appear symmetrically either side of the central line. If they don't, it means that your drawing is out of balance. You have plenty of opportunity for drawing ellipses in this exercise so try to make them as accurate as you can. Check that none of the curves look odd or out of proportion.

Have a go at drawing the same object from a slightly different angle. This gives you both practice at drawing and familiarizes you with its overall shape. Having drawn it a couple of times, do it again from another viewpoint, so that you get even more information about the object. All this concentration on one object boosts your knowledge of the world of 'form', which is essential for an artist. You can repeat the exercise as many times as possible with different objects, knowing that the more you draw the better you will become.

Working Up a Simple Object

Now you can start to portray objects in a little more detail, adding some tone to lend solidity. First I have chosen a cup and saucer, because this pair of closely fitting objects is fairly simple to draw, but sufficiently complex to be a good test of your newly acquired skills.

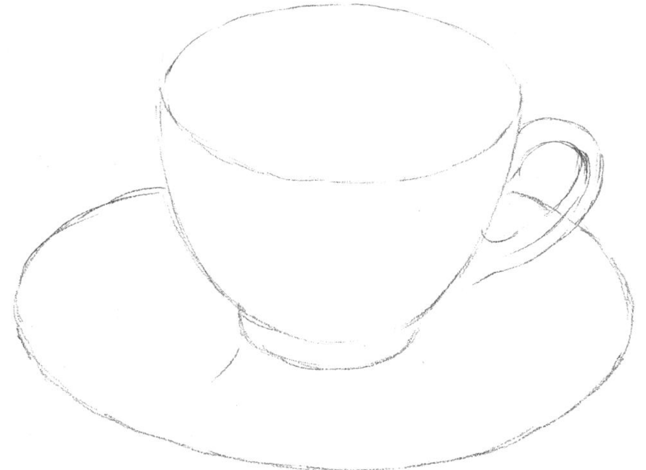

1. First draw the ellipses to show the top and bottom of the cup, and the main shape of the saucer. Draw the handle shape and the curved sides of the cup.

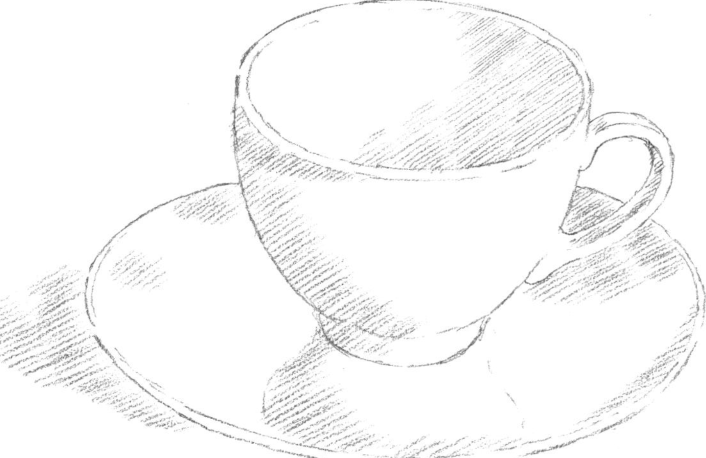

2. Add in the main areas of shade with, as before, one single tone. Pay attention to the inside of the cup and to the tones on the side of the saucer.

3. Lastly, work up the tones until you get a good likeness of the shape and reflections on the objects.

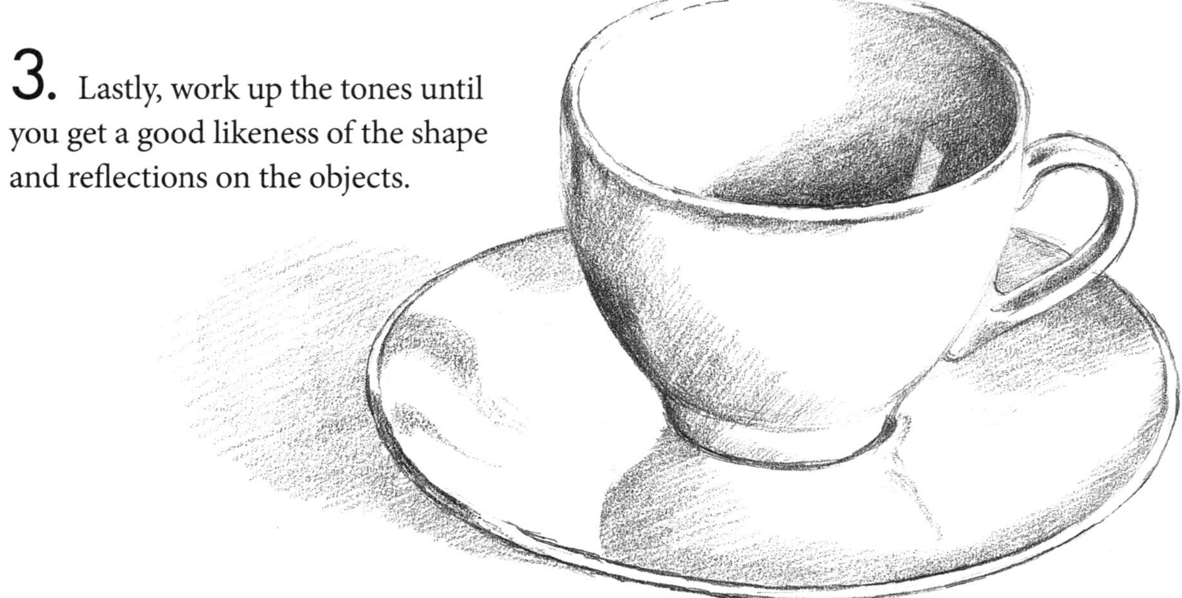

The next object is a glass jar containing tinted water.

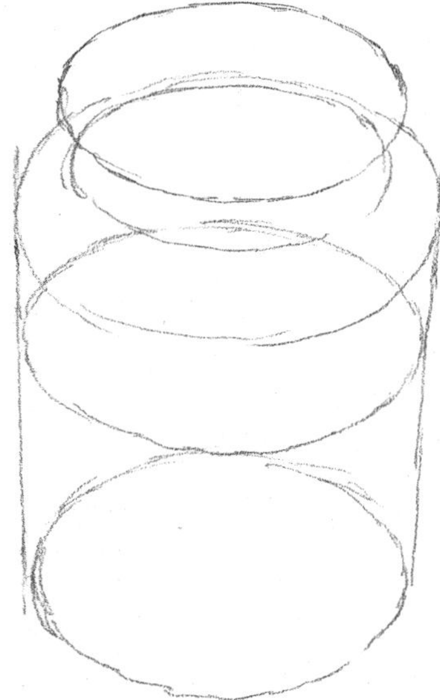

1. As before, draw the ellipses and outside edges of the jar, not forgetting to indicate the level of the water as well.

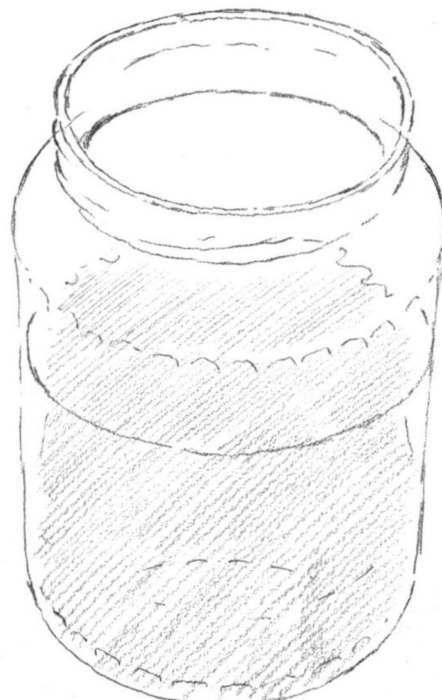

2. Shade in the area that represents the tinted water. There will not be many other tones, due to the transparency of the glass.

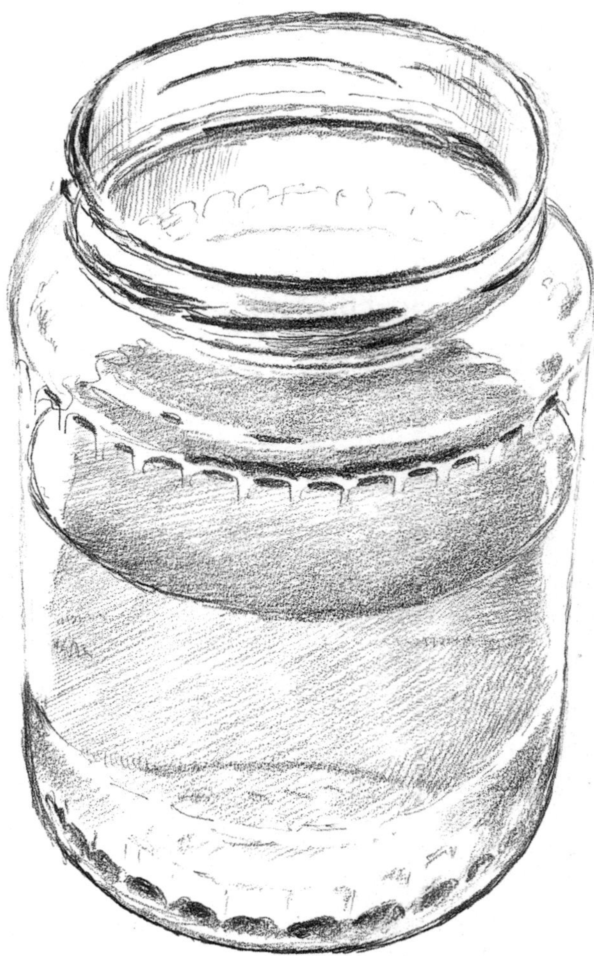

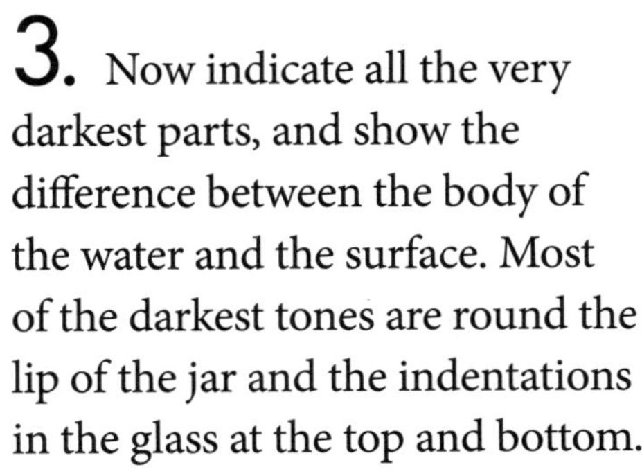

3. Now indicate all the very darkest parts, and show the difference between the body of the water and the surface. Most of the darkest tones are round the lip of the jar and the indentations in the glass at the top and bottom.

Tone On an Object

It is only once tone has been added that an object begins to look like something three-dimensional that you can handle and use. The following drawings show just how important it is to be able to use tone to describe the substance of objects.

1. In this drawing I've drawn a light-coloured jug, first in outline to show how the shape alone, if well described, will give you quite a lot of information about the jug. You can see that it must be round and that it has a lip and a handle, and it appears to be on a surface, the limit of which you can see behind it.

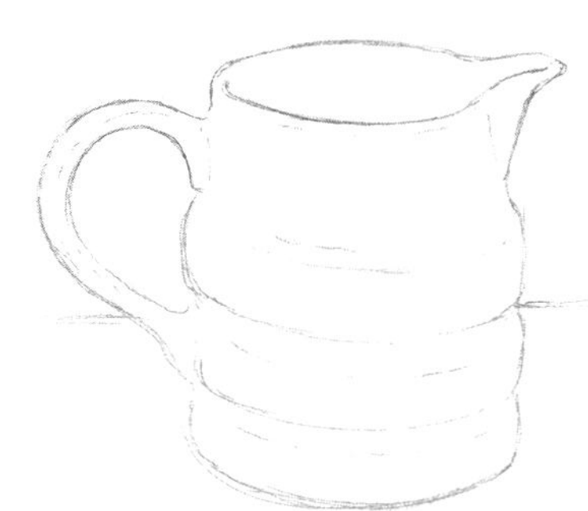

2. Here all the tone has been put in to show the difference that this makes to our knowledge about the object. The space is more defined and the quality of the curve of the jug is more clearly seen. The object looks solid.

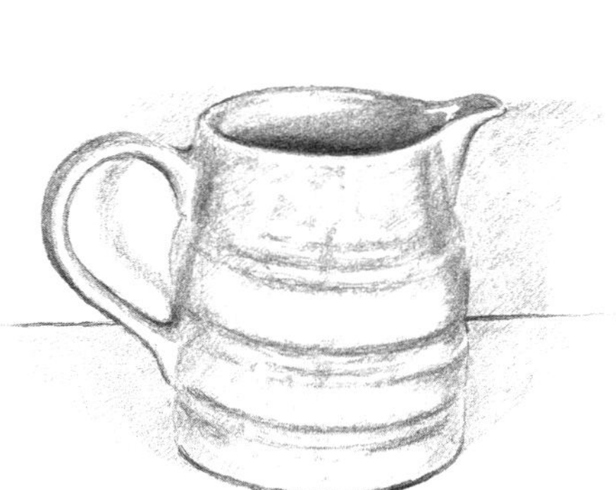

3. In the next drawing I have put in all the tone on the jug but have left out the tonal background. This has the effect of making it appear to float in the space, because it doesn't have any real connection with the background.

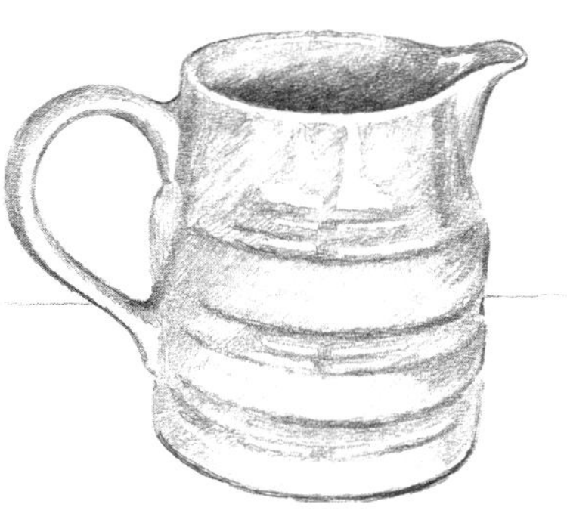

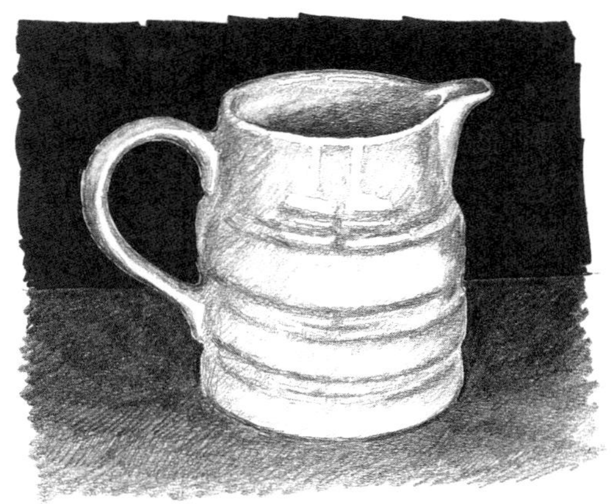

4. The last drawing of the jug does the opposite, making the dimensions of the object loom out of the darkness of the background, so that it's very clearly defined as light against dark. This isn't realistic, but it's a good way of bringing our attention to the jug shape jumping out of the space. So you can see that tone can add or subtract from your drawing.

Having looked at some of the possibilities of tone, we can now turn our attention to some straightforward objects on which you can practise your technique. Take this opportunity to try using some different materials and experiment with the effects you can achieve.

First, a drawing in ink of an apple. The build-up of tonal texture is done in a scribble technique, which seems to work well with round objects.

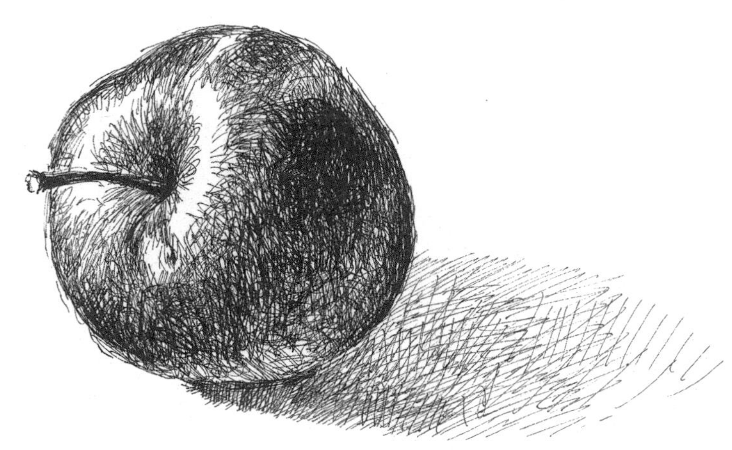

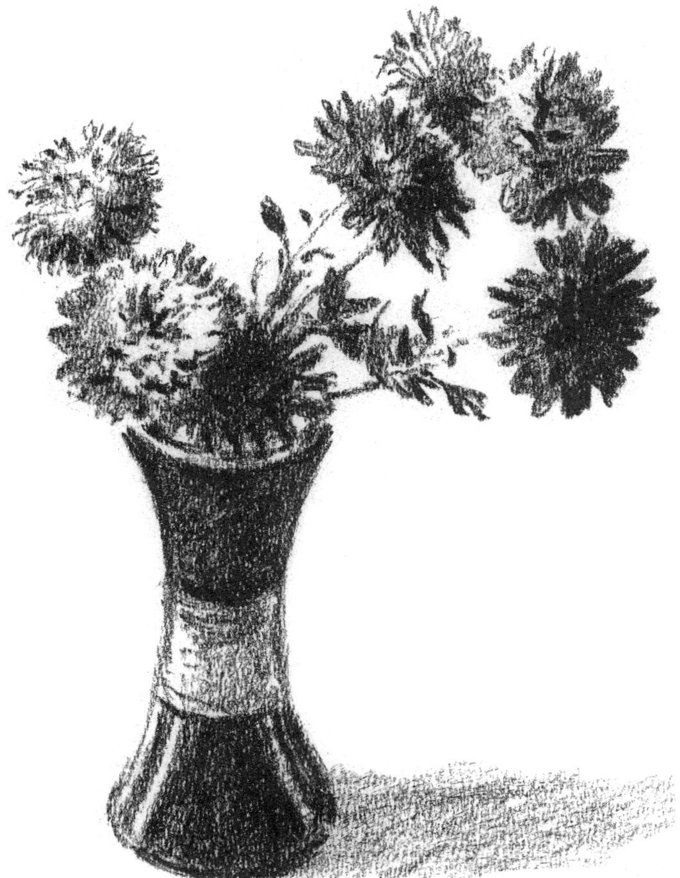

These flowers are drawn in charcoal. The soft edges of the medium suit the quality of the plants. The slightly fluffy texture of the blossoms is easily shown in this medium.

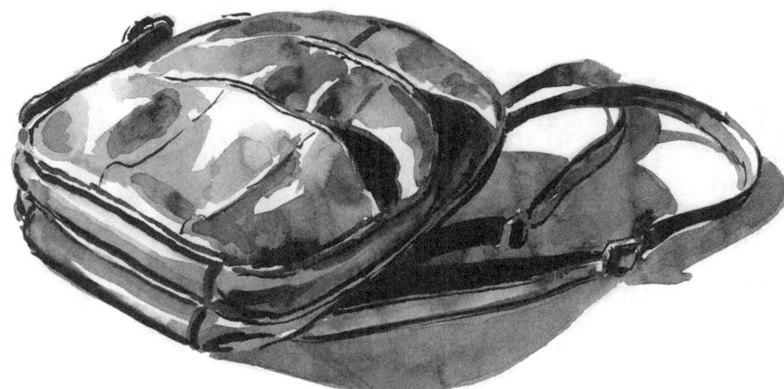

The brush and wash technique is appropriate for this drawing of a leather bag as it emphasizes its slightly squashy appearance.

Concentrating On One Thing

For this drawing practice, concentrate on one thing for a certain period of time. You don't have to complete all the drawing in one go; instead try spending two or three days on it. Take a mundane object which has a little complexity about it, such as a shoe. This item of clothing is familiar enough and very basic, but also quite a strange shape once you begin to study it.

1. First of all, draw the shoe from a side view. Notice the proportion of length to height and rough out your drawing in order to get this right. Then draw it with as much detail as you can, ignoring nothing about the texture and shape of it. Keep correcting as you go along and take the drawing as far as you can in the time available.

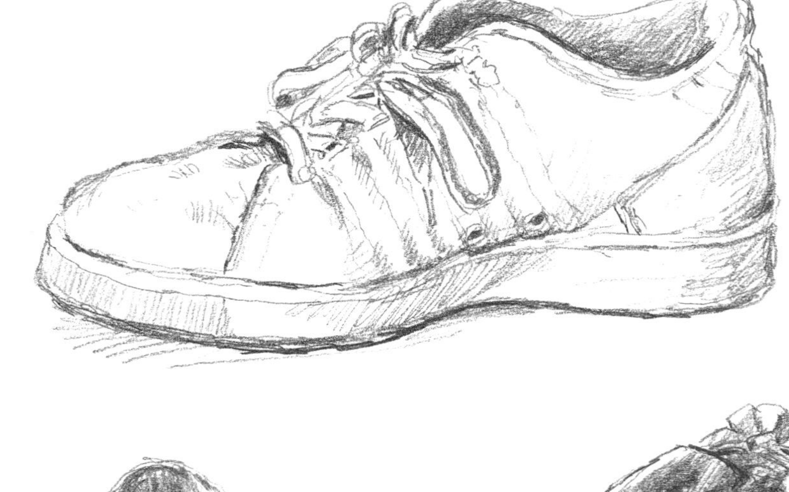

2. When the first drawing is complete, draw the shoe with the toe pointing towards you. Once again rough out the main shape, getting the proportions right. If there are shoelaces, tie them in a bow to keep them within the main shape. Once again, draw every detail, making corrections as you go. When your drawing is as good as you can get it, put it away until you are ready to draw again.

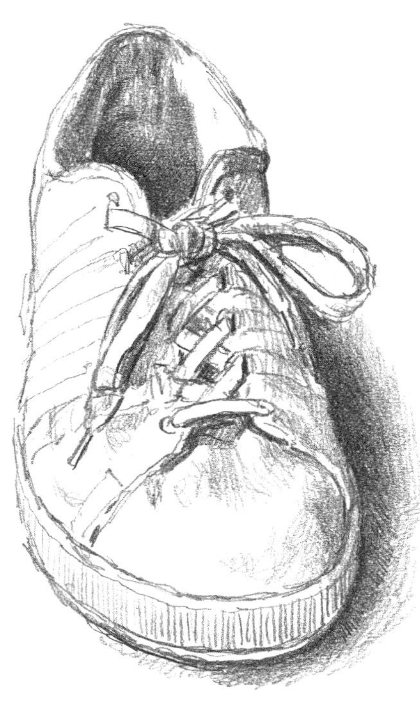

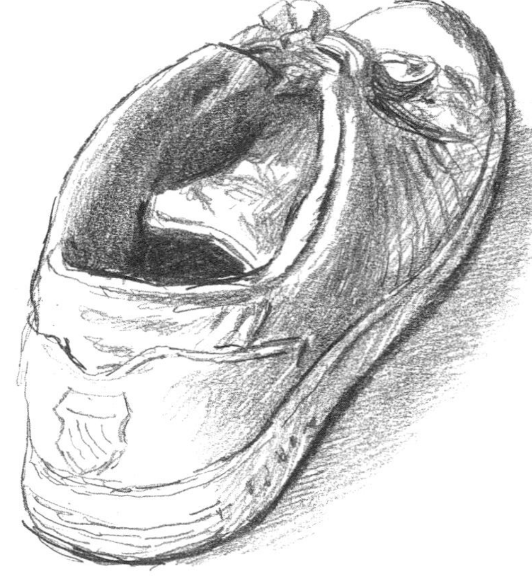

3. Now have another go at the shoe, this time with the heel towards you, and proceed just as you did before. This may seem a bit obsessive, but it's the easiest way to improve your drawing abilities.

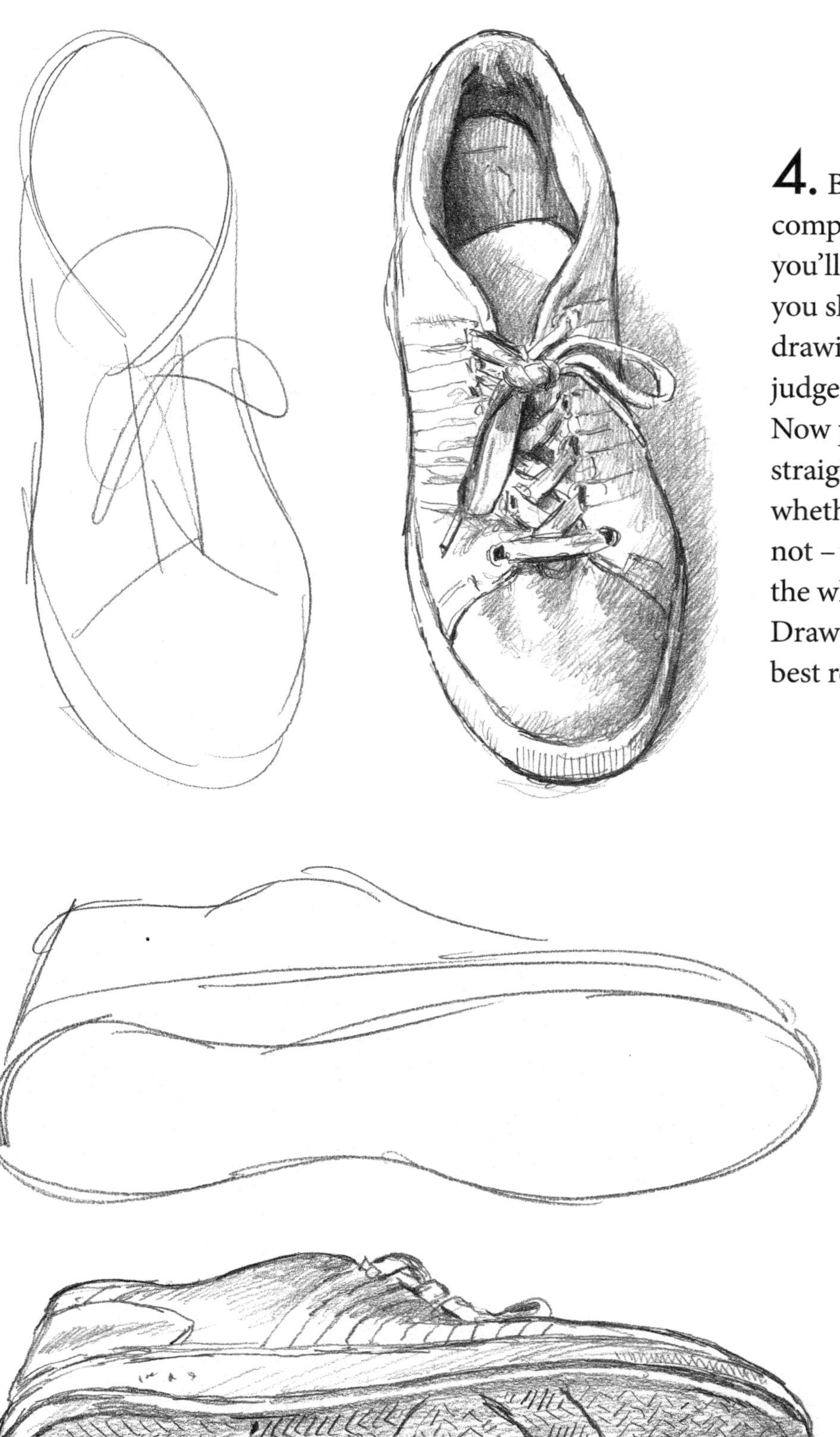

4. Before you make the next drawing, compare the three you've done. This way you'll spot what has worked well and what you should avoid repeating in the next drawing; this process also helps you to judge your own work more objectively. Now place the shoe so that you can look straight down into it. It doesn't matter whether you have the toe towards you or not – the main thing is to be able to see the whole shape of the shoe from above. Draw it as before, working towards the best result you can get.

5. Finally, draw the shoe with the sole towards you. This is quite challenging: it's the least obvious way to draw a shoe, so you'll have to be on the alert for unusual angles. When you're satisfied, spread the drawings out so that you can see them all together. You'll now know that you're capable of a body of work that exhausts all the possibilities of drawing a shoe. This is good for your artistic memory, because although you may not come to draw a shoe for some time, the memory will help you whenever you do have to draw one. All the drawing that you spend concentrated time on will help to inform your later work.

Larger Shapes

Now let's look at some bigger objects. We start with an ordinary iron garden chair that's not only very traditional, but also, in this case, fairly old and worn. The chair's linear shape means that it is ideal for this practice.

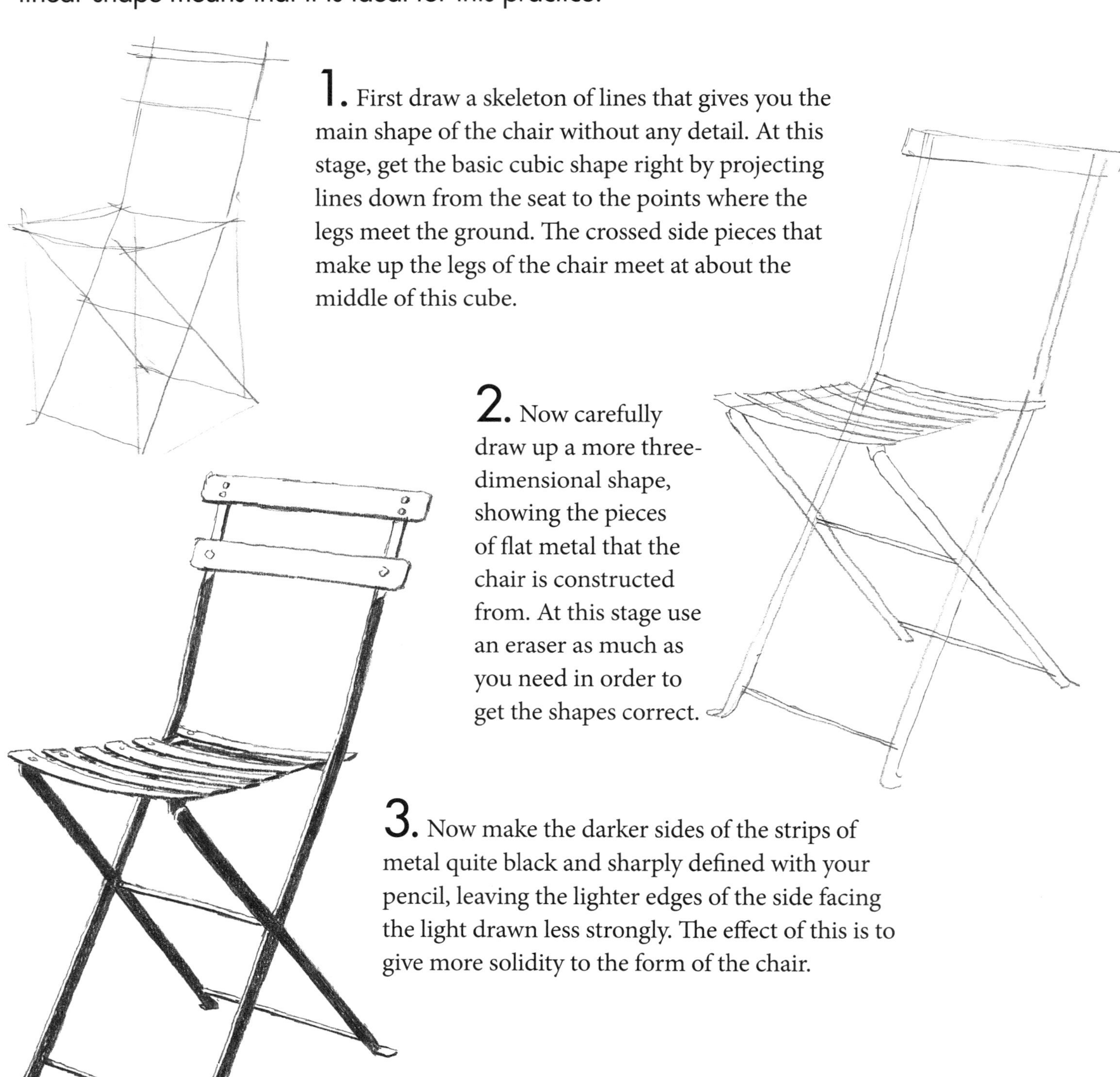

1. First draw a skeleton of lines that gives you the main shape of the chair without any detail. At this stage, get the basic cubic shape right by projecting lines down from the seat to the points where the legs meet the ground. The crossed side pieces that make up the legs of the chair meet at about the middle of this cube.

2. Now carefully draw up a more three-dimensional shape, showing the pieces of flat metal that the chair is constructed from. At this stage use an eraser as much as you need in order to get the shapes correct.

3. Now make the darker sides of the strips of metal quite black and sharply defined with your pencil, leaving the lighter edges of the side facing the light drawn less strongly. The effect of this is to give more solidity to the form of the chair.

Keeping Up With the Joneses

Now try your hand at drawing one of our largest man-made domestic objects. There are plenty of cars around even if you don't have one yourself; I got tired of drawing my own, so I went out and found the one with the most interesting shape in our neighbourhood.

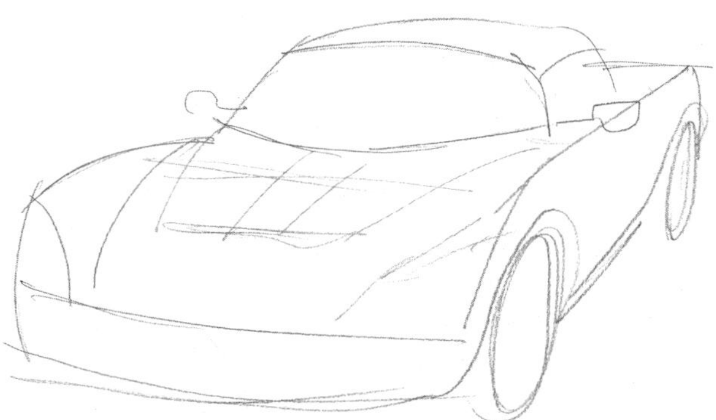

1. First pick a good angle from which to draw the car. I chose an almost front-on view, but go for the one you think is the most interesting. Get the main shape down first, defining the most obvious features of the vehicle, not forgetting the wheels. Take your time over this, it is worth getting the shape reasonably correct and well-proportioned before you start adding the details.

2. When you are satisfied with the shape of your vehicle, simply mark out all the main sections and then begin to shade in the key tonal areas. This might not be too easy, as the reflections on the polished metal and glass can be quite complicated to represent on paper.

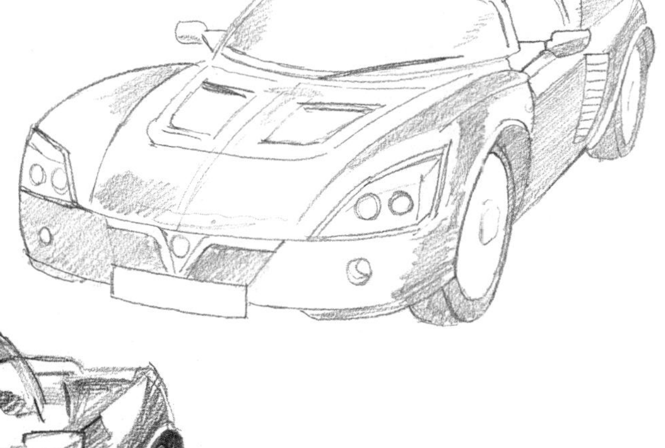

3. Once the main tonal areas have been completed, put in as many details of shape and tone as you can – for instance on the radiator, grill, lights and wheel hubs – making sure that the full tonal range is included, from the very darkest to the brightest highlight.

Materiality

Showing some awareness of the material constitution of your still-life subjects will make your final drawing all the more convincing. There are well-known ways of drawing that make materiality quite clear. Here are some examples.

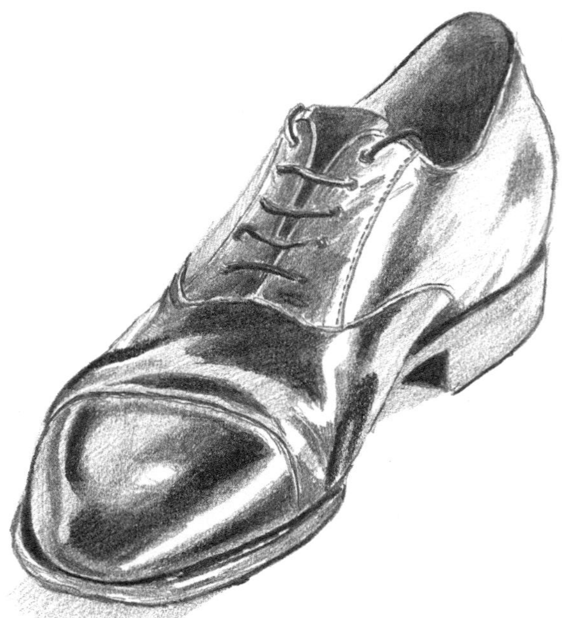

Leather – matt or shined

This particular shoe is dark and well polished, so there are strong contrasts between the light and dark areas. Study it carefully and observe how those light and dark areas define the shape of the shoe, as well as its materiality. Notice how the very darkest tones are often right next to the very lightest, giving maximum contrast.

Glass – what makes this glass look convincing?

The shape of this tumbler, set against a dark background, is defined by the glass picking up all sorts of reflections from the surrounding area. Notice how a section of the straight edge behind the glass is visible but in a distorted (refracted) way, because of the thickness of the material and its curved surface. Make sure that when you draw the outline of the glass it is well delineated, because this outer shape holds together the rather amorphous forms of the reflections. Also, note how the brightest highlights occur in only one or two small areas. Don't be tempted to put in too many highlights or the tumbler won't look so transparent.

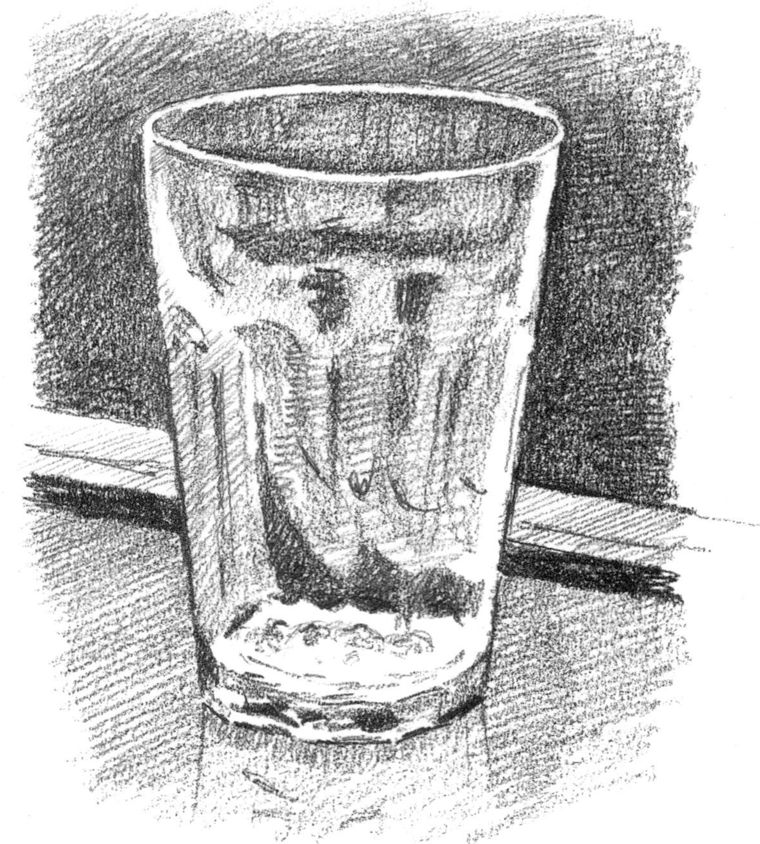

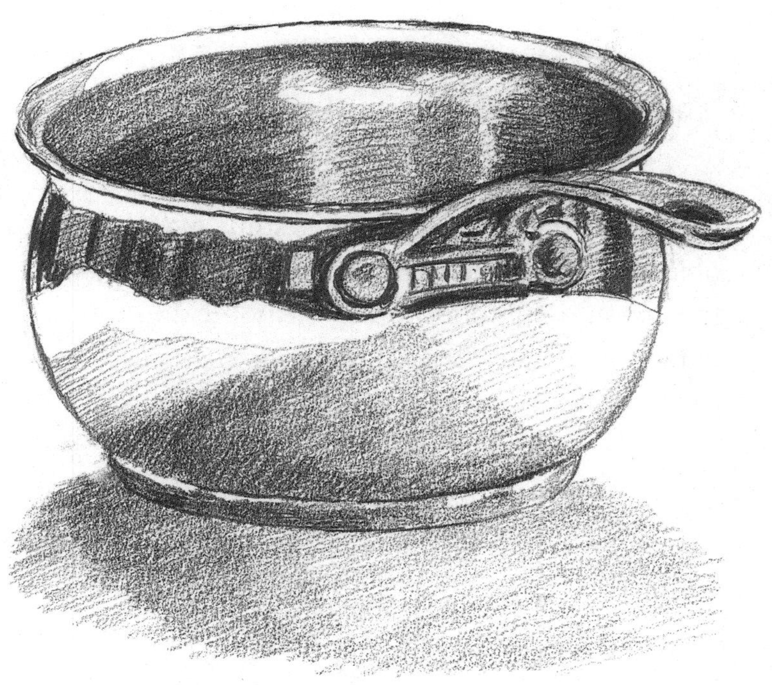

Metal – strong reflections

The metal object I have chosen is also a highly reflective piece of hardware – a shiny saucepan. Once you have drawn the shape as accurately as you can, you have to decide how much of its reflectivity you are going to show. As we saw with the car on page 21, reflections on this type of surface can become very complicated to draw, so it is reasonable to simplify them to a certain extent. Make sure you represent all the main areas of dark and light and that, once again, the very brightest is placed next to the very darkest. The interior of the pan is not so clearly reflective and you should show the difference between the inside and the outside. The cast shadow is also important because this is reflected in the side of the pan and reinforces the illusion.

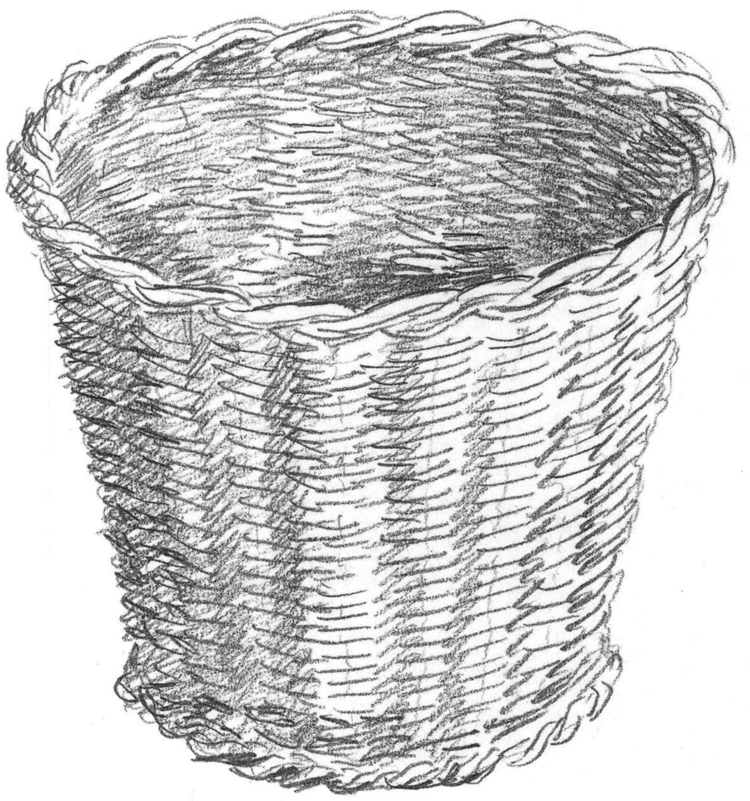

Basketwork – strong texture

This particular texture needs careful drawing in order to achieve the best general effect. On the plus side, the shapes of the woven strands of basket are repetitive in nature, so once you get the hang of it, it should not take you long. When the pattern of the basketwork has been completed, the shadow on the inner part and down one side should yield a three-dimensional aspect.

Pottery – hard and smooth

This pottery bottle shouldn't be too difficult to draw because the surface is not as reflective as some of the previous objects and the shape is simple enough. Just make sure that the gradation of tone around the bottle doesn't look too harsh, and create a little texture with pencil strokes round the contours to mimic the striated surface.

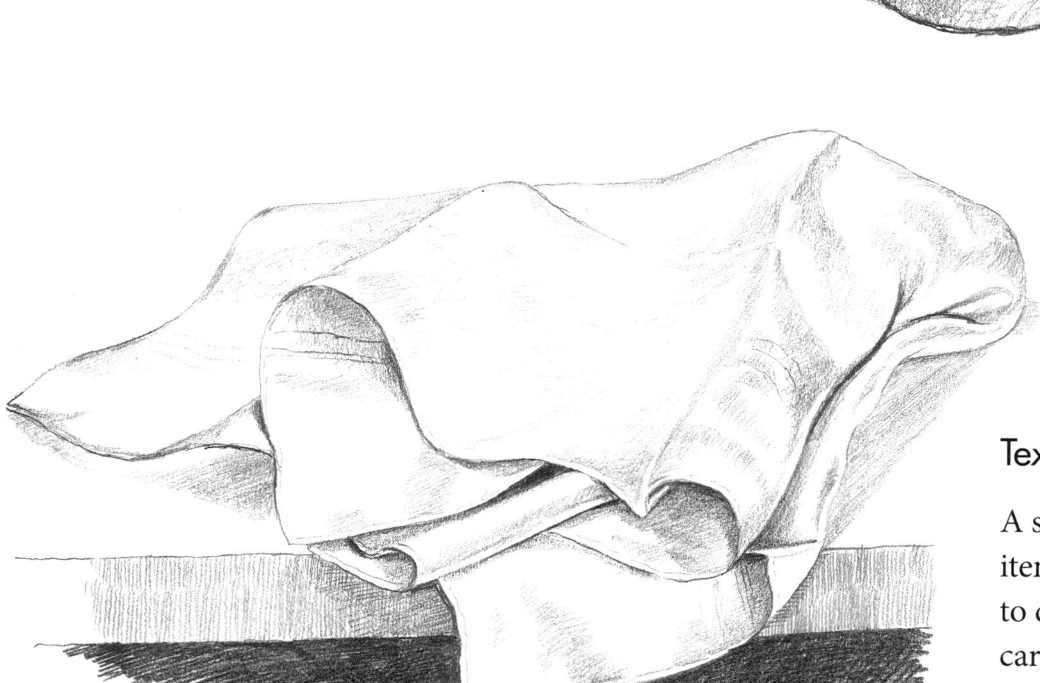

Textiles: silk – soft surface

A silk handkerchief is the next item and, again, is not so difficult to draw, although it does require careful rendering in even tones. Folds occurring in silk fabric tend to be rounder and softer than in any other material.

Textiles: corduroy – tough texture

This corduroy shirt is made of a fairly stiff material and this quality should show in the way you draw the folds. It also has a distinctive surface texture, which makes it look very different from other, smoother fabrics. Don't delineate every detail of the surface, just the shadowy areas where the tone is deeper.

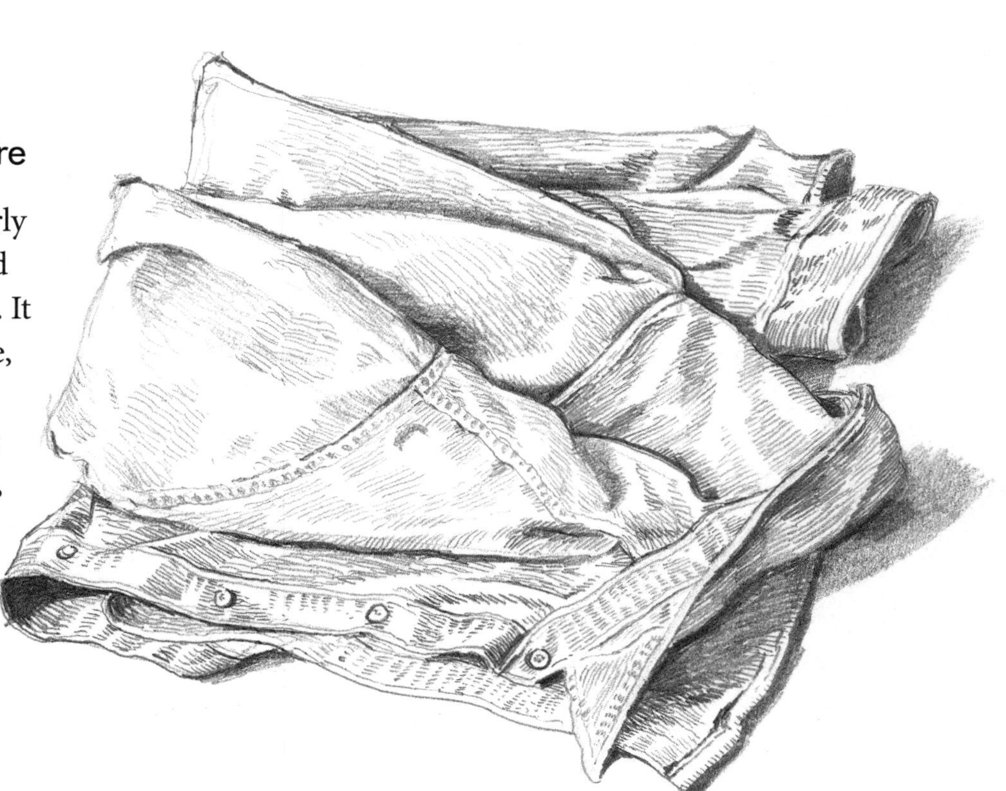

Paper – crumpled surfaces

Unlike most of the fabrics we wear, crumpled up paper exhibits quite sharp folds. This is the chief way to differentiate it from textiles. The other characteristic of paper is that it reflects light well, and consequently there are very few deep shadows.

Vegetables – draw what you eat

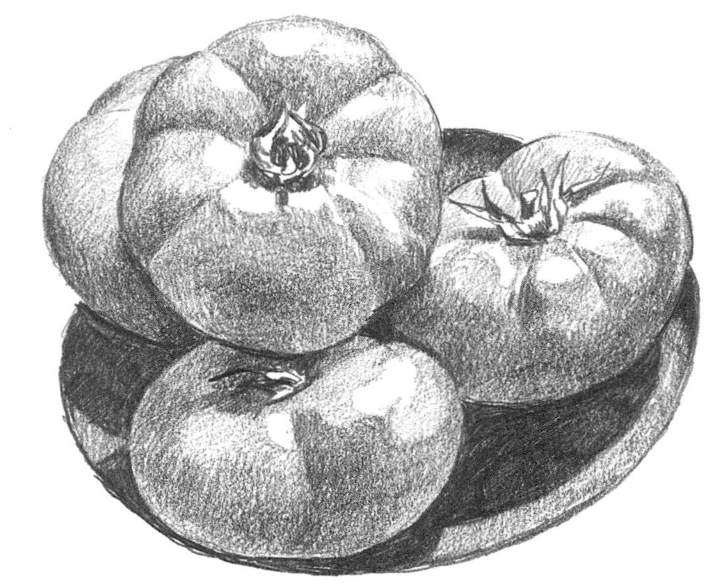

Fruit and vegetables are great standbys for still-life artists, and here we show a couple of examples. The bowl of tomatoes gives an idea of the smooth shiny surface of the fruit. The main aim here is to balance the dark and light tones to give a convincing impression of the curved surface.

The cauliflower is an altogether different proposition, with strongly veined leaves and a creamy, lumpy 'curd'. No part of the surface of the vegetable is smooth and you need to show a strong contrast between the dark leaves and the white flowers.

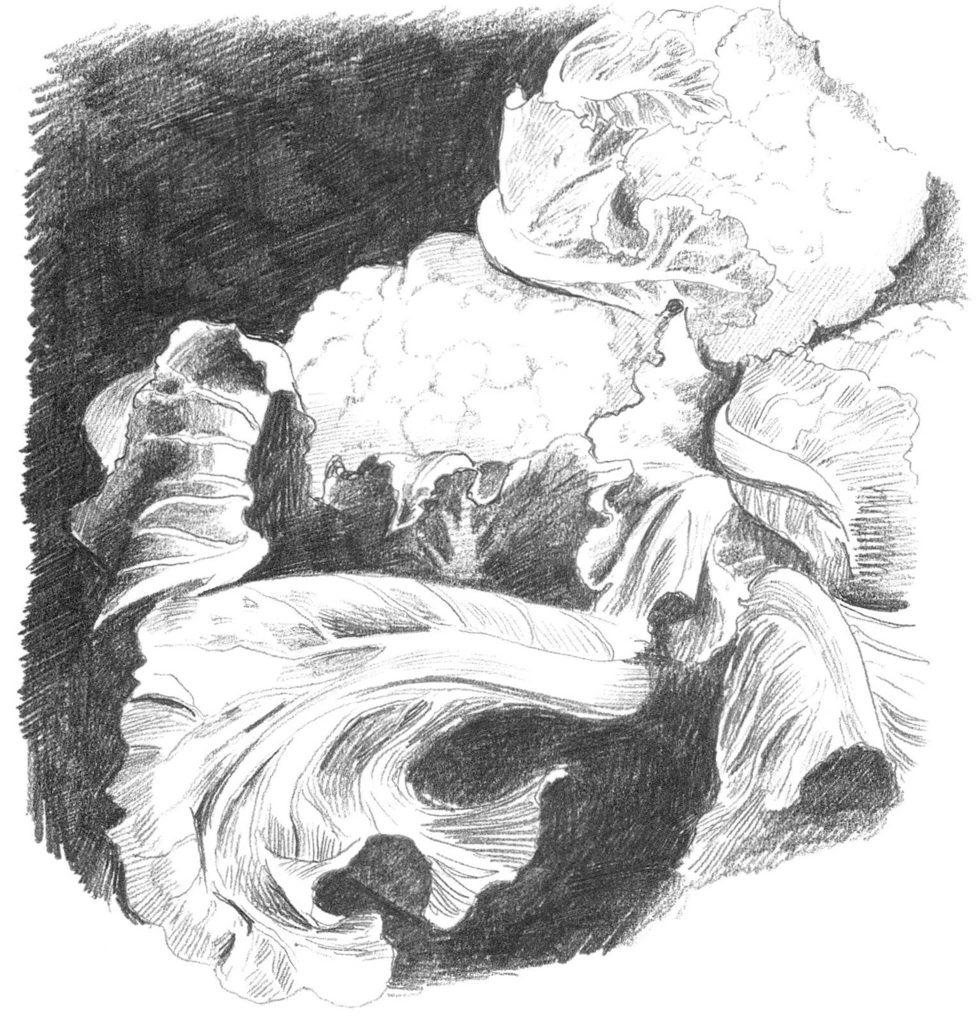

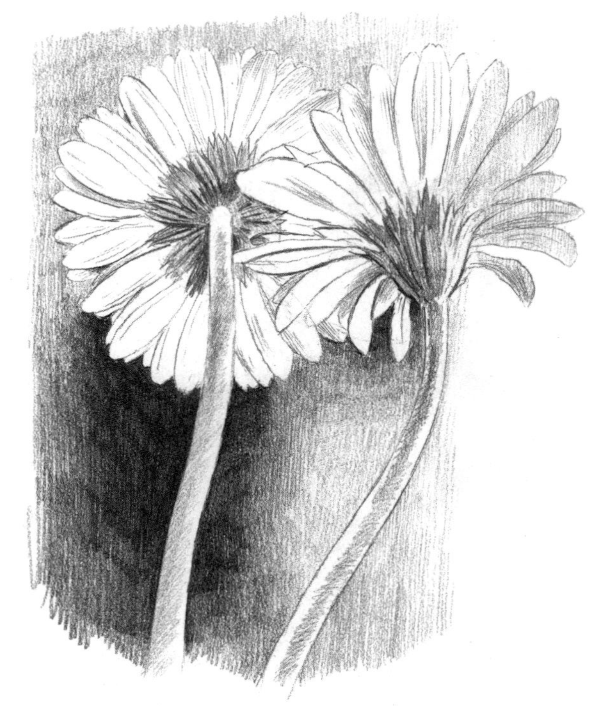

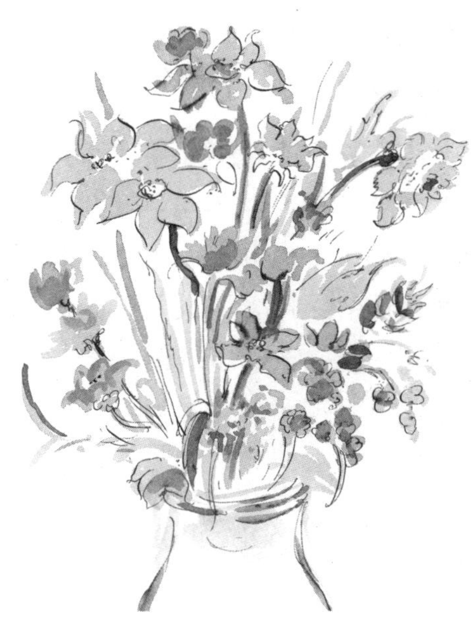

Flowers – different methods

Here are two approaches to try when drawing plants.

For the first (above left), take a big close-up of a boldly shaped flower and draw it in as much detail as possible. Keep it big.

Then, for contrast (above), try something like a vase of flowers and draw them in very lightly with sweeping strokes. Don't worry about the details, but concentrate on getting the flowing feel of the growth and the fragility of the flowers. Here less is more, in that you don't want to overdraw your subject, so keep your marks very loose and impressionistic.

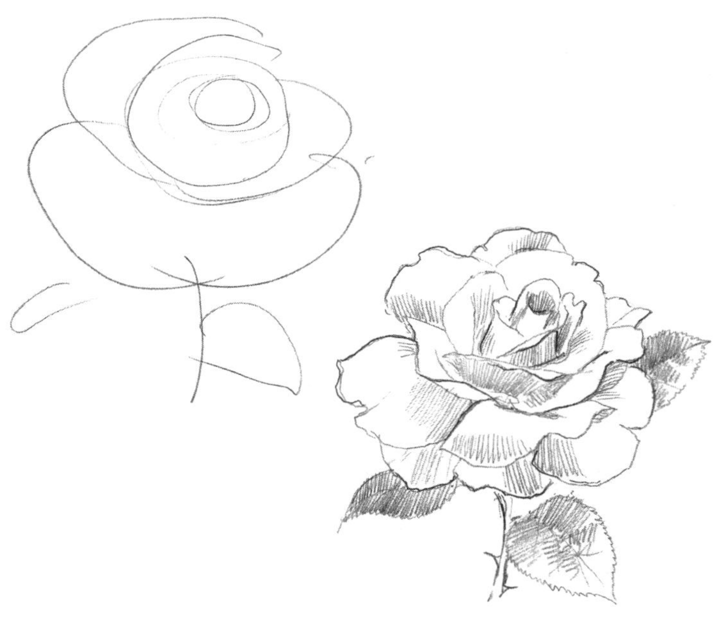

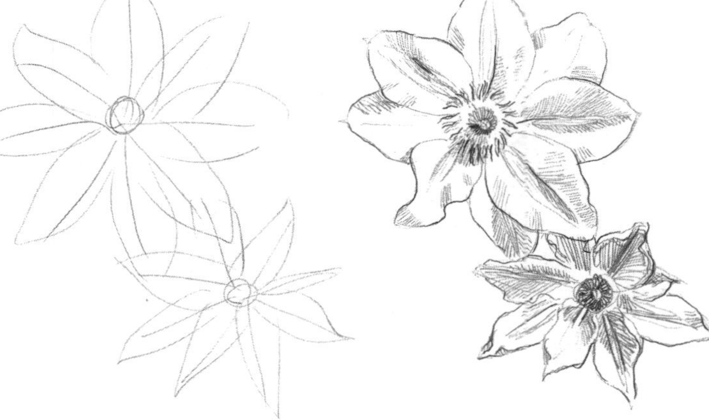

These rose and clematis flowers present interesting and complex shapes and need to be carefully studied in order to render their delicate texture.

Simple Still Lifes

It isn't difficult to put together a still-life arrangement, but it does require some thought and aesthetic appreciation. If you are a beginner, it's a good idea to accumulate your still-life objects gradually, with some feeling for how the final shape of the arrangement will look. I began by choosing things that make interesting drawing problems for an artist to solve.

Starting with what happened to be on the top of the plan chest in my studio, I gave myself the problem of drawing a number of pencils bunched together in a glass jar. I had to find a way of showing the transparency of the pot and the variety of pencil tops poking up out of it – slightly difficult, but not so much so it would become laborious.

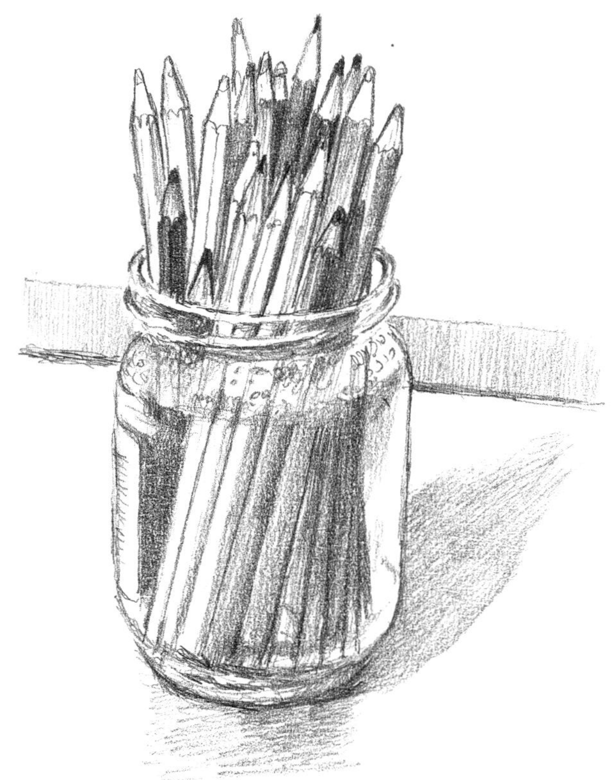

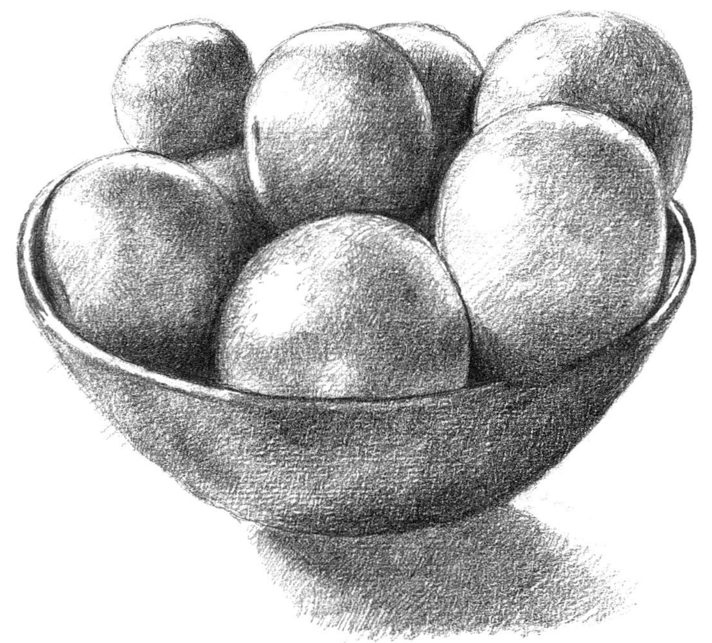

Next I took a bowl of oranges that was on my dresser. Fruit in a bowl is a traditional prop for still-life arrangements and presents the problem of drawing spherical objects that are pushed together by the sides of the bowl.

Both of these subjects can successfully be used to make a simple still life without any other objects being necessary; of course you might want a bit more background space to show off the quality of your drawing, but nothing else is needed.

I then drew a glass vase with one stalk of flowers in it. This is both a simple and complex subject, because while there is only one flower and one vase, the latter is glass, which can be difficult to draw convincingly, and the flower is a composite stalk of many small blossoms. There are two stages to portraying the subject – first the simple outline of the shape and then the building up of tonal values so that the finished piece looks as though it exists in its own space.

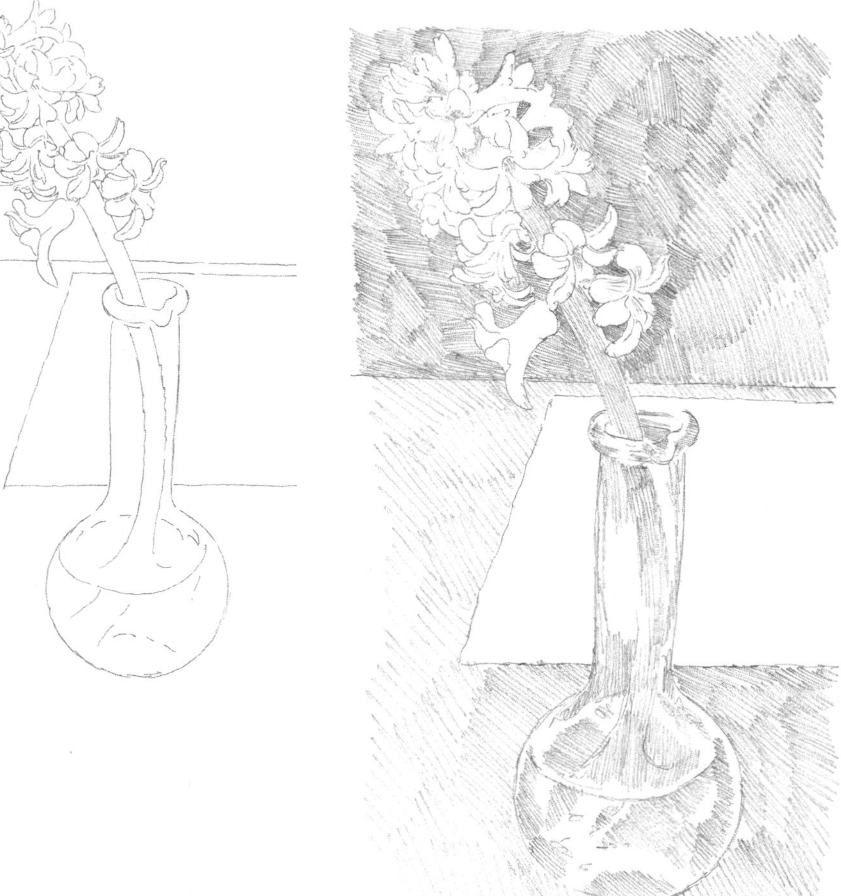

First make a light tone over all the areas where the shading will be, leaving untouched white paper for the highlights.

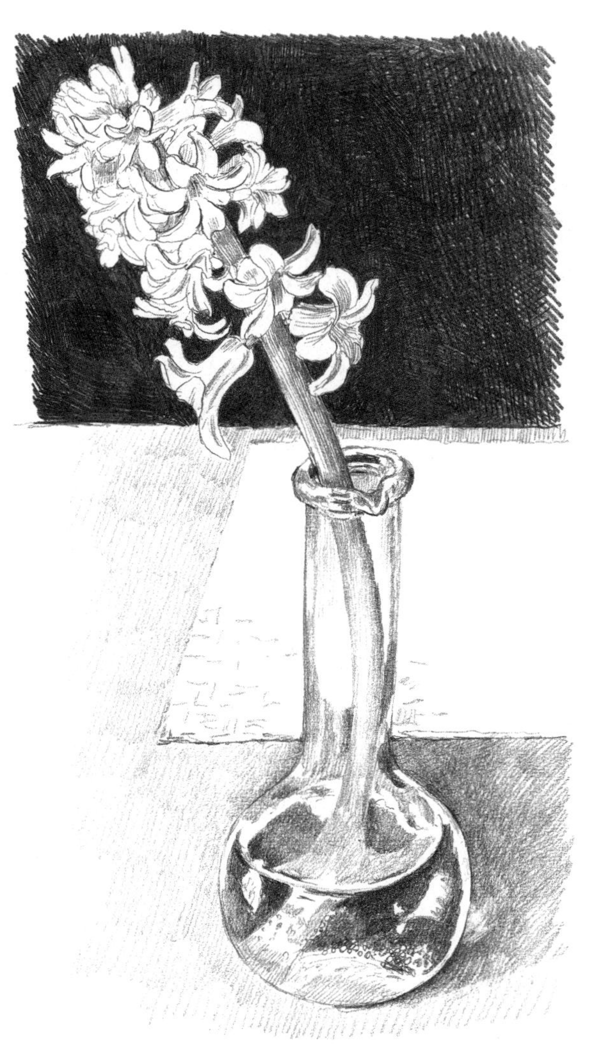

Following this, build up more varied depths of tone to give the objects substance. Note how I have placed the flowers against a dark background to show up their brightness. The glass vase has a much lighter background in order to make the drawing of the glass simpler. Draw all the distortions that the water and glass produce to give a convincing impression of their qualities.

Accidental and Composed Arrangements

The still-life objects on these two pages were just sitting there waiting for someone to notice how interesting they were. This is one of the benefits of drawing still life – you begin to see subjects everywhere you look. You may wish to make slight alterations to obtain the composition you are after, or you can simply draw the arrangements as they are.

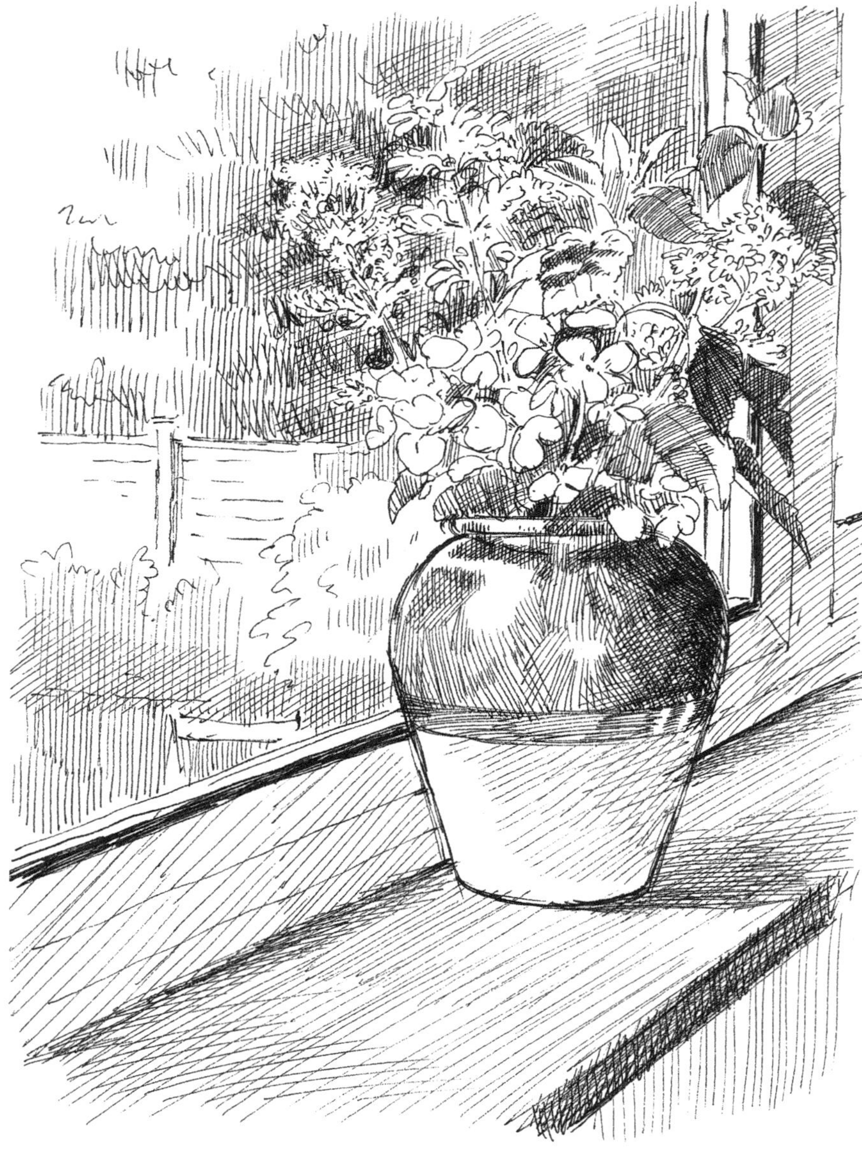

Here is a vase of flowers on a windowsill. You can see the perspective of the surface it is standing on, the way the light from outside lights up the objects, and the background of the garden through the window pane.

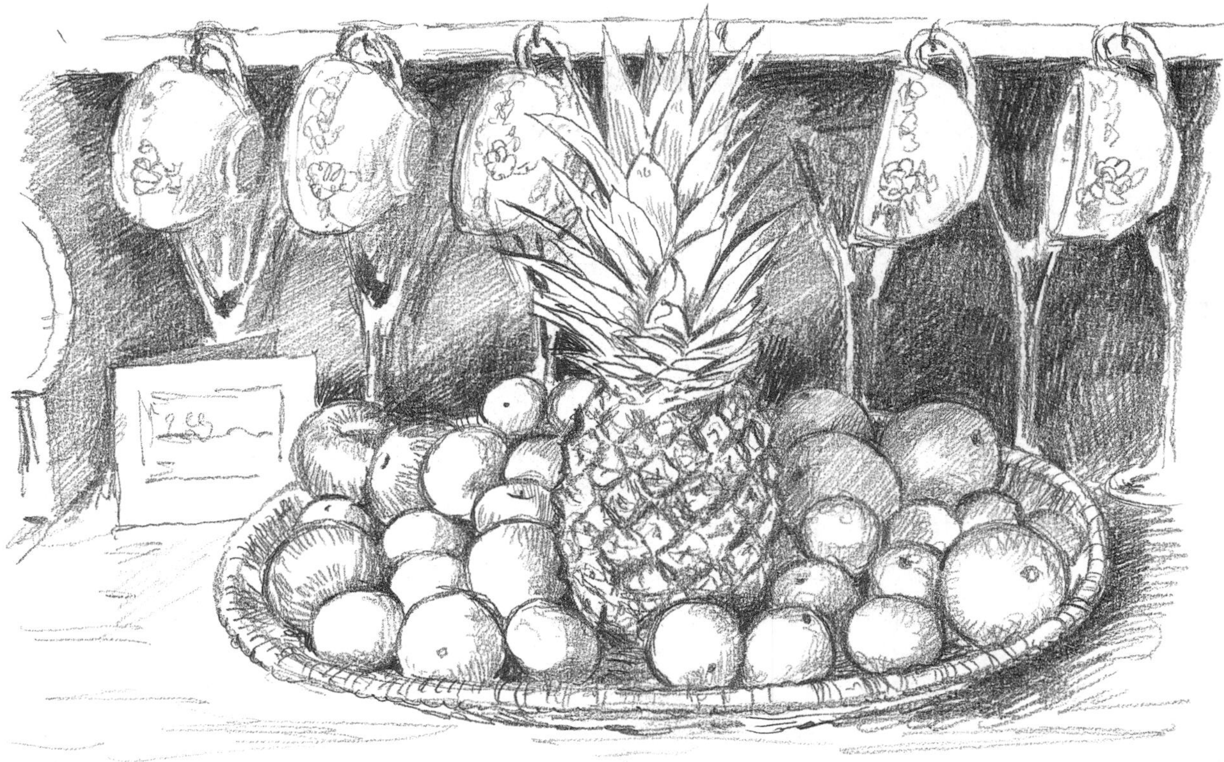

The next composition is much more complicated. It consists of several cups hanging on a sideboard, glasses under the shelf and a large basketwork tray full of fruit, arranged fairly carefully. This is much more like the traditional paintings of still lifes that artists have been making for many generations.

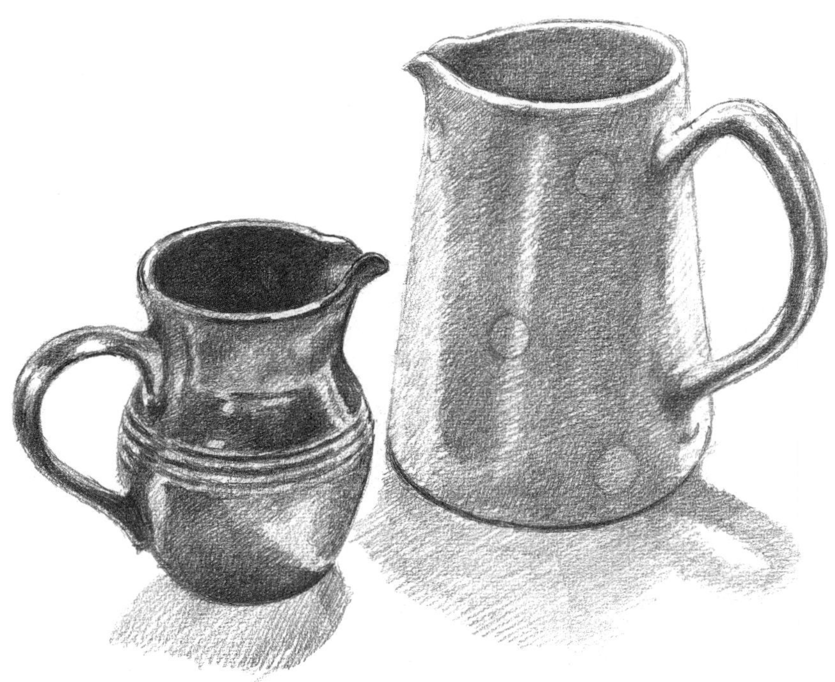

The next choice was more considered. I found two jugs of different shapes and sizes and placed them next to each other, turning them so that their spouts were facing. The fact that one is short, curvy and dark in colour while the other is tall, straight and lighter figured in my reasons for choosing them. This demonstrates how you can make aesthetic judgements about even a very simple subject, whereas in the two previous examples I had just happened upon the still lifes.

Ephemeral Still Lifes

One of the attractions of still life is the simple, domestic scene it often portrays: the tea-tray, a coat thrown over a chair. Even the most simple drawing can catch the feeling of a house or home.

Here is a kitchen still-life composition in a tall format, seen against the light coming from a nearby window. It is rather quickly drawn and looks as though it is probably a temporary arrangement.

A tea setting is the next arrangement, in its simplest form of just a cup and saucer, teapot and milk jug. This is something you might see in any home.

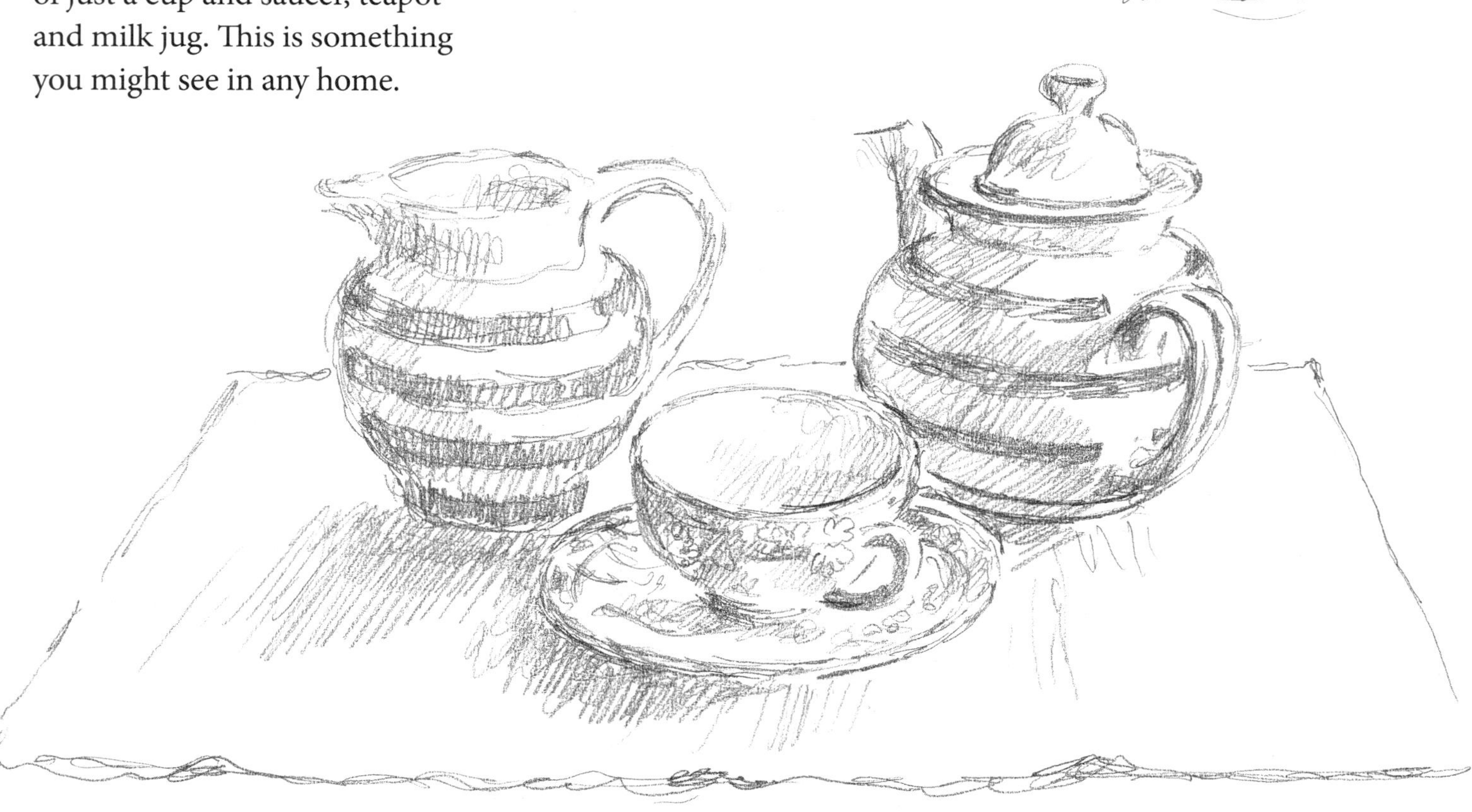

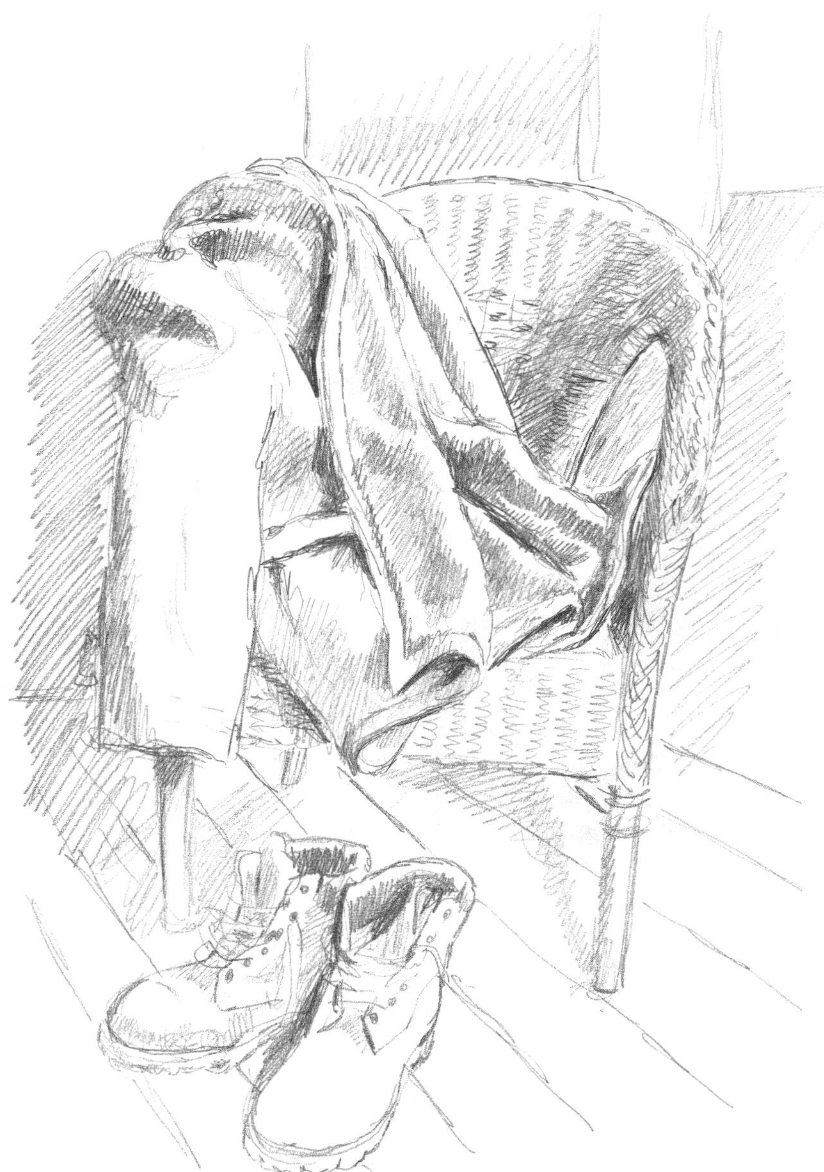

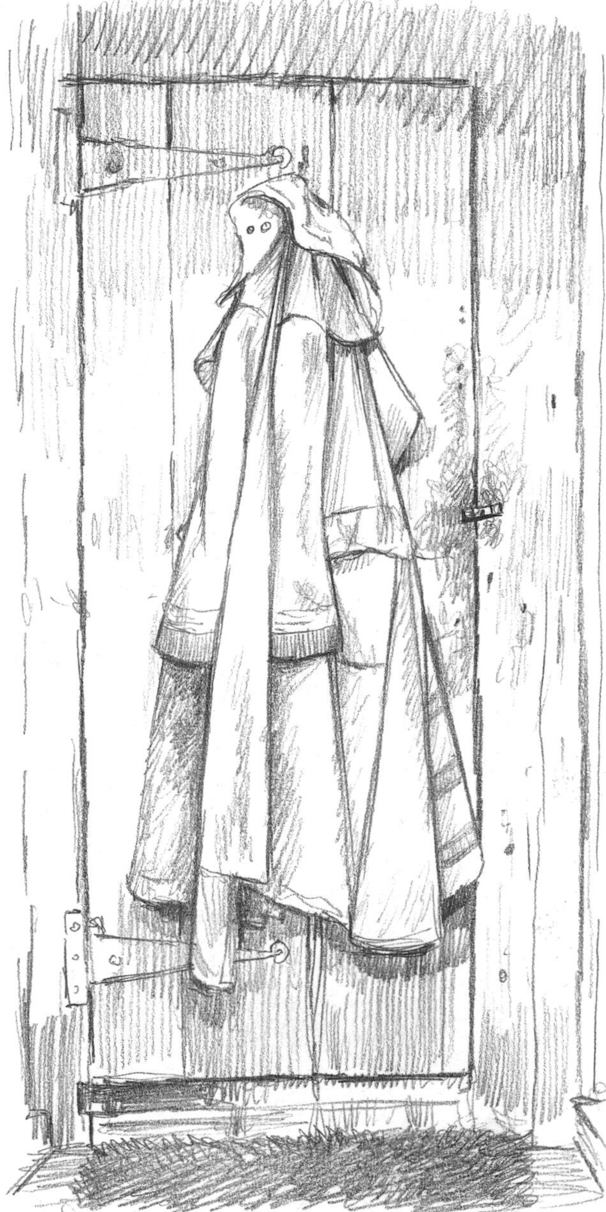

Then we see two still-life arrangements that use the effect of clothing in the scene. On the right is a door, probably outside, with an old heavy garment like an overcoat hanging on it. Above, a heavy coat is thrown over a basketwork chair and a pair of heavy boots stand on the floor nearby. They look as though they might be picked up at any moment.

Negative Shapes

In a drawing there are no spaces as such – the shapes between and around objects are just as important as the shapes of the objects themselves. These 'spaces between' are called negative shapes, and when it comes to creating more complex compositions involving several objects, observing them will help you to draw more accurately.

Here is a still life group, which you may want to draw. Your first instinct will probably be to try to draw it object by object, hoping that they will relate to one another correctly.

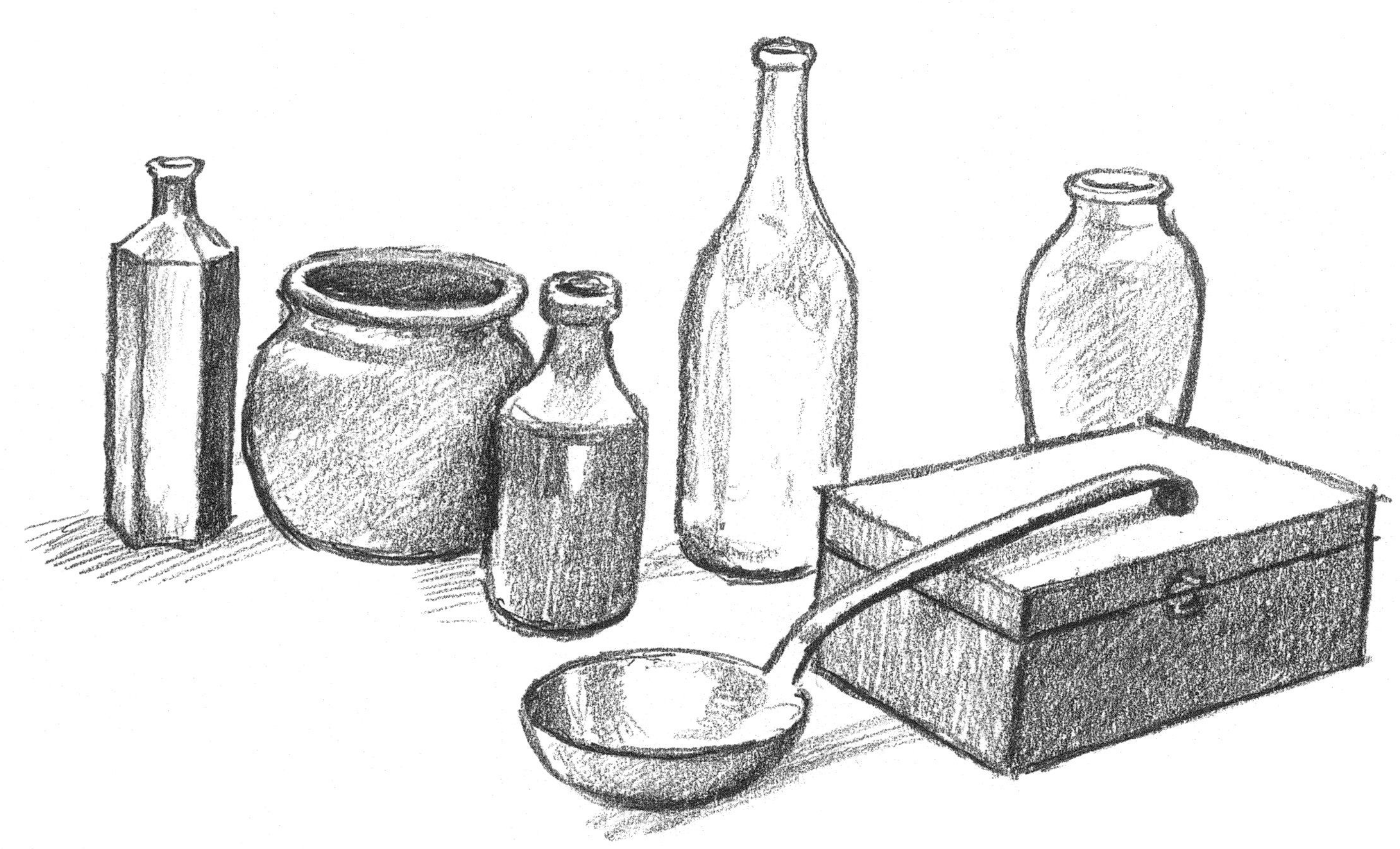

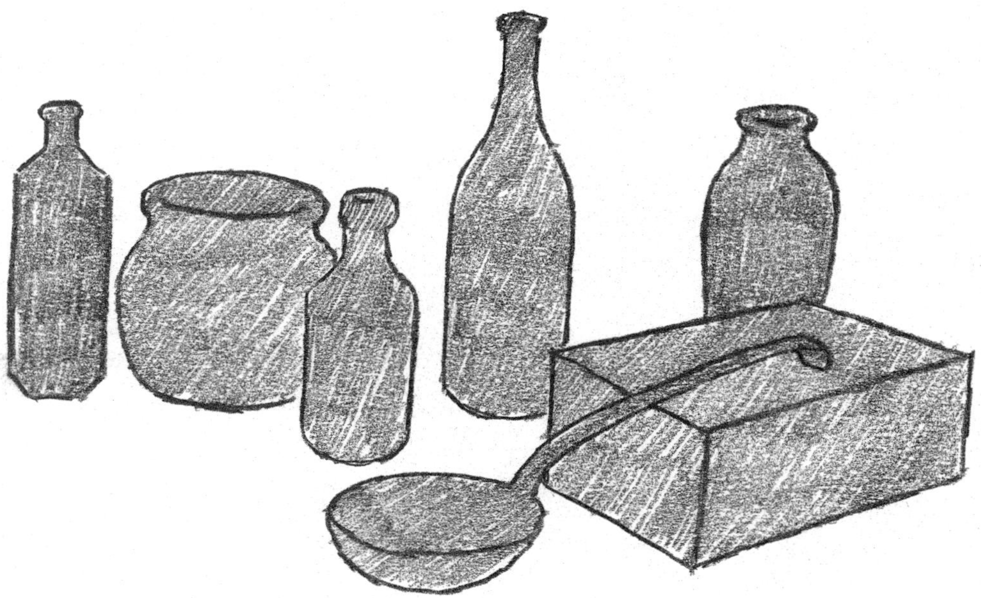

Seeing the group of objects drawn in a flat tone helps you to understand the positive shapes and their relation to one another.

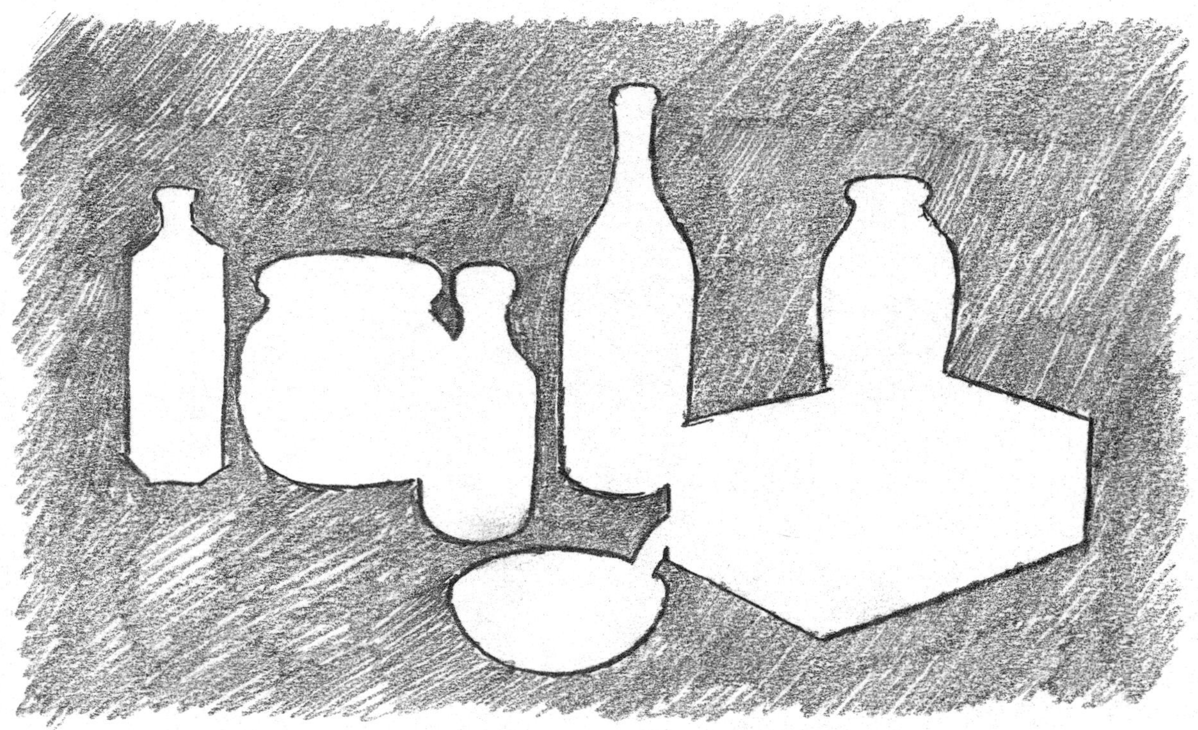

In the example above, you can see how drawing the negative shapes describes the forms of the objects and how much they overlap one another.

Master Examples

You can learn a huge amount by studying the work of professional artists from all eras. Here are four still-life compositions that, although simple, are carefully thought out and executed.

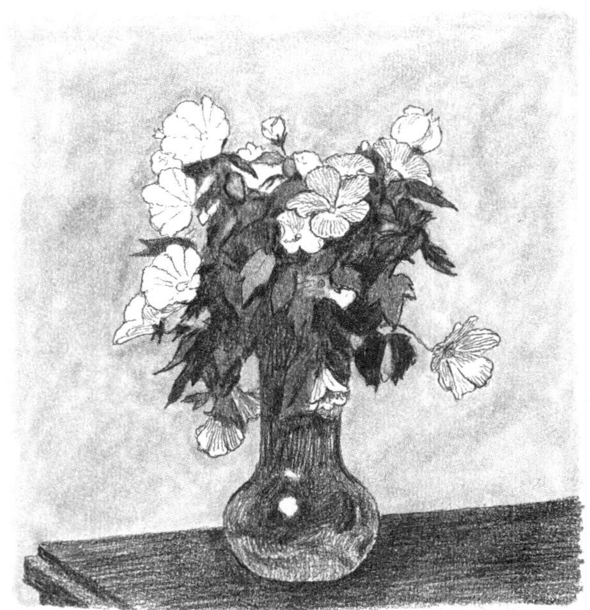

Above is a still life that's simple enough in composition, although it's not easy to achieve this degree of sensitivity. The main thing to notice is just how carefully Henri Fantin-Latour (1836–1904) puts in the various tones of the leaves, all of which are darker than the flowers. The contrast between the flowers and the leaves, the jar and the tabletop, gives a feel of the fragile quality of the blossoms.

In the piece below, William Brooker (1918–83) has approached the theme in his inimitable way. He has placed the vase with the single rose on the edge of a table, with a well-ironed cloth making a strong triangle shape below it at the corner of the table. He has kept his tonal areas very simple, almost flat, so that the composition has an almost abstract feel to it. This cool, dispassionate look at an ordinary theme makes it less ordinary.

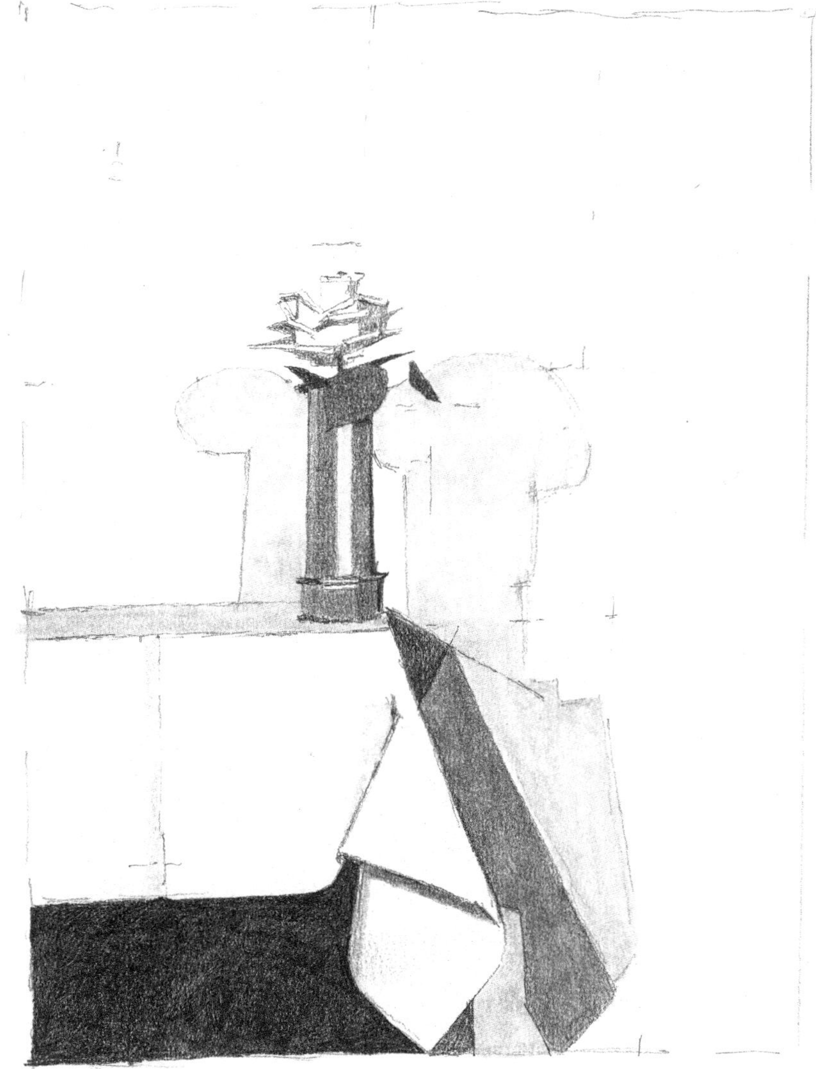

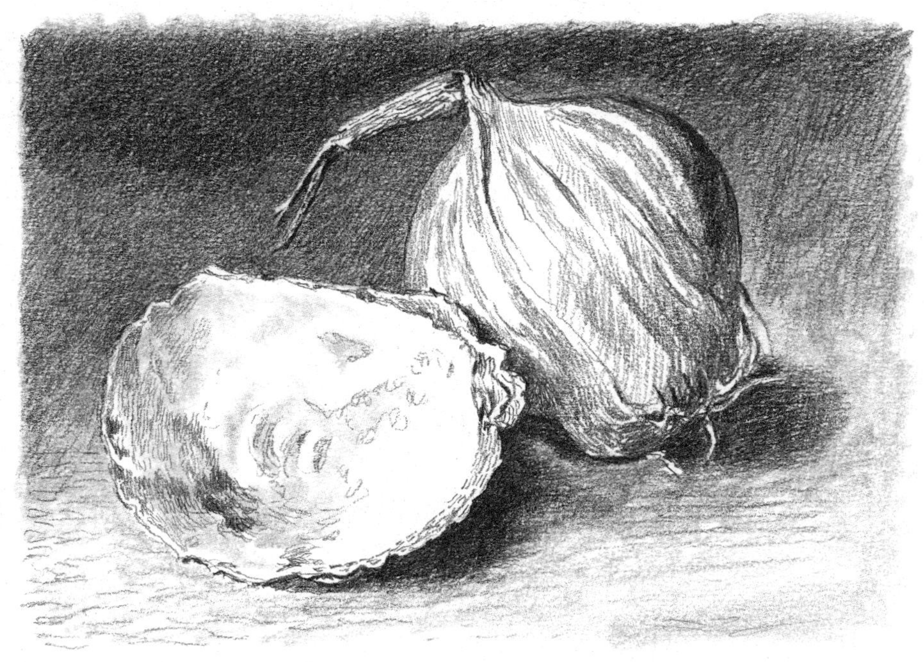

Here William Henry Hunt (1790–1864) has placed an oyster shell and a large onion close together on a surface with a darker background. He makes the most of the different textures of the two subjects, so that as a study in materiality it is quite powerful. This is always a good way to approach a simple still life as it intensifies the viewer's experience.

This example is after William Nicholson (1872–1949). Here the artist shows a jug and a beaker lit strongly from the left against a lighter background. Because of the strong light, the objects almost disappear against the background, with only the strong painted markings on their surfaces giving them some substance. Limiting the objects in this way increases the intensity with which the still life can be viewed.

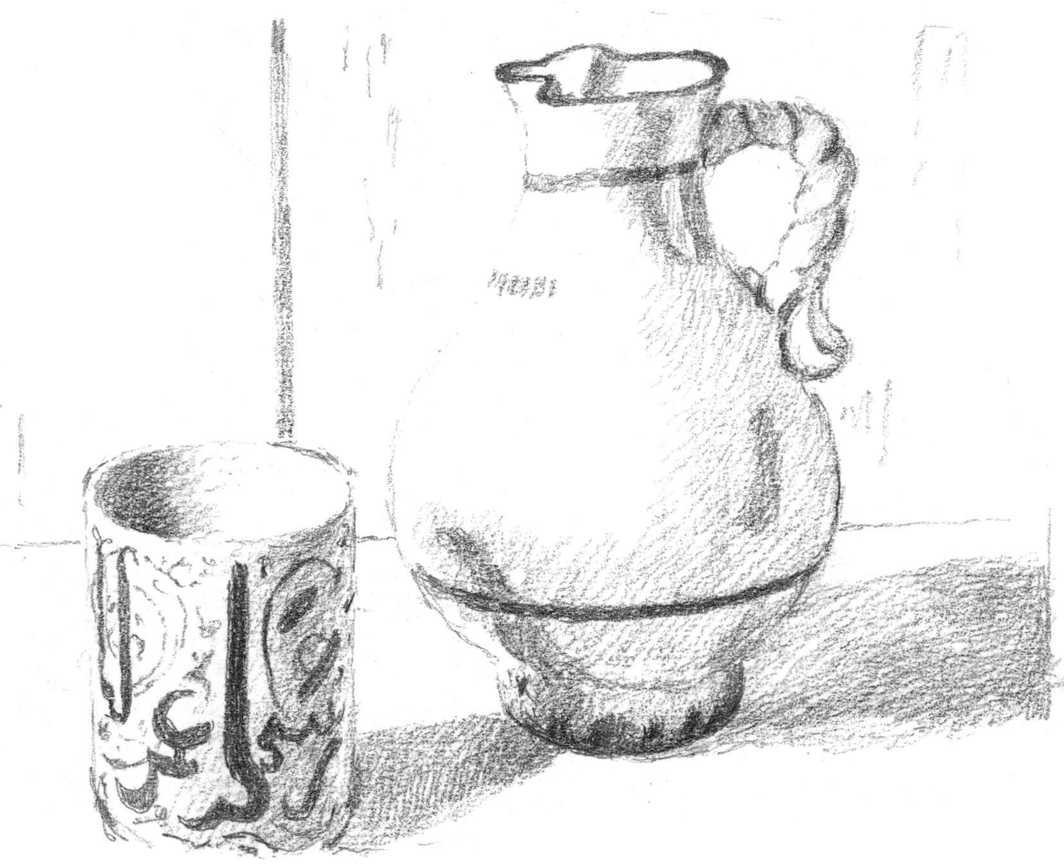

A Still-life Project

The drawings on these pages show how you might go about selecting a still-life subject. Remember to take some time to work out your ideas before you choose a composition and progress through the stages to a finished piece of work.

Choosing your subject

The first step is to look around your home and contemplate the different possibilities. I began by walking out into the garden near my studio and, seeing an old watering can, I just started drawing it. It didn't at this stage suggest a composition to me, but it was a good start to the search for objects for the still life.

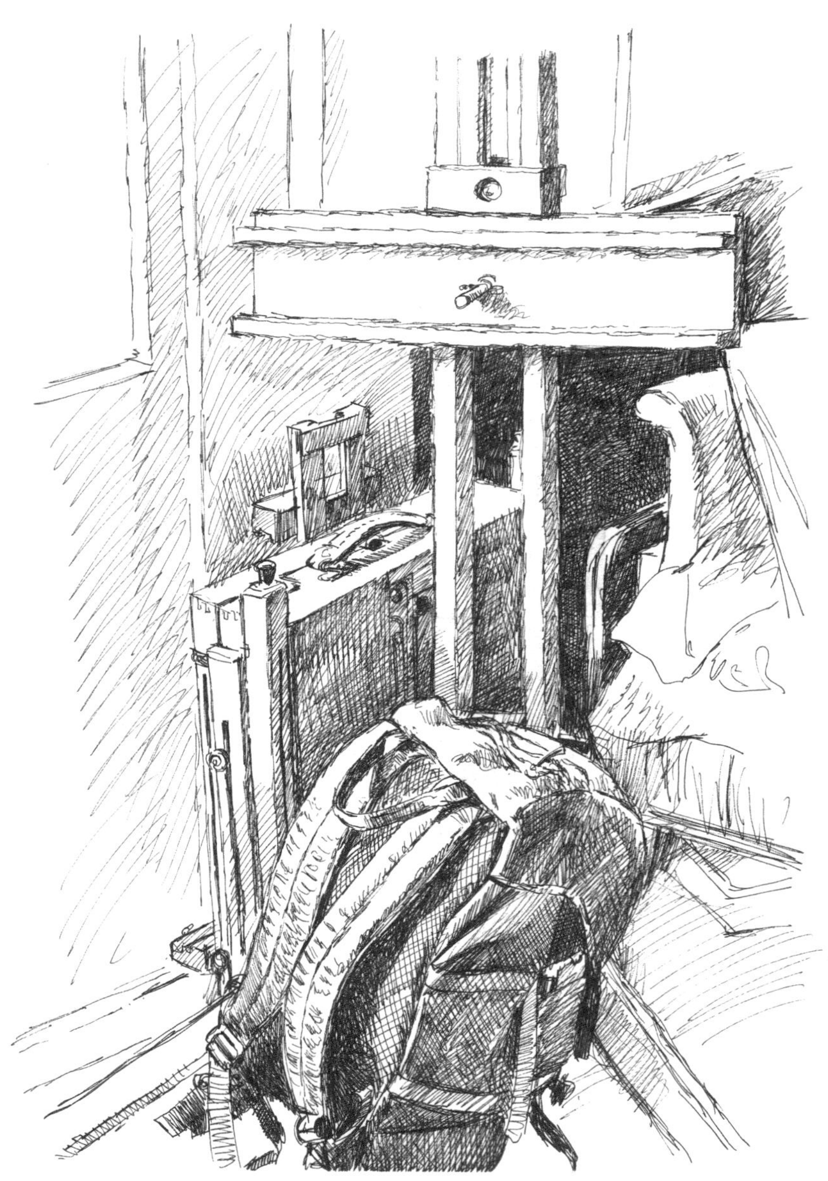

Back inside my studio, I considered the easel in one corner with a box-easel behind it and a rucksack full of painting kit propped up against it. This made an interesting subject, but it was not quite varied enough for my taste.

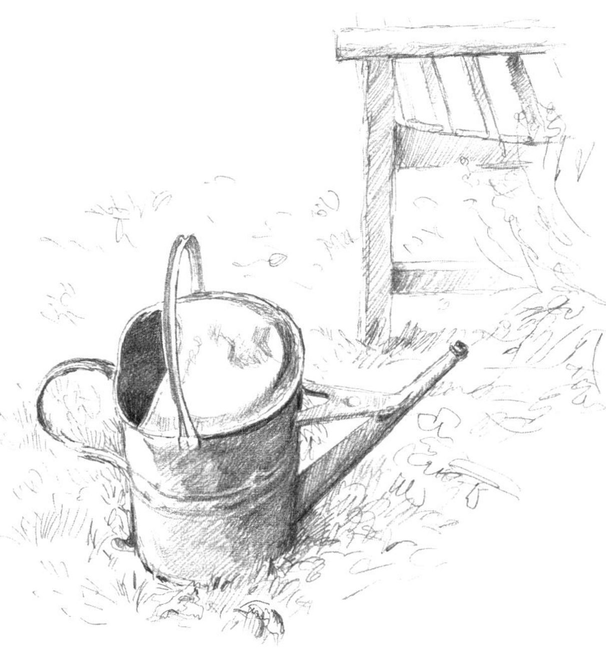

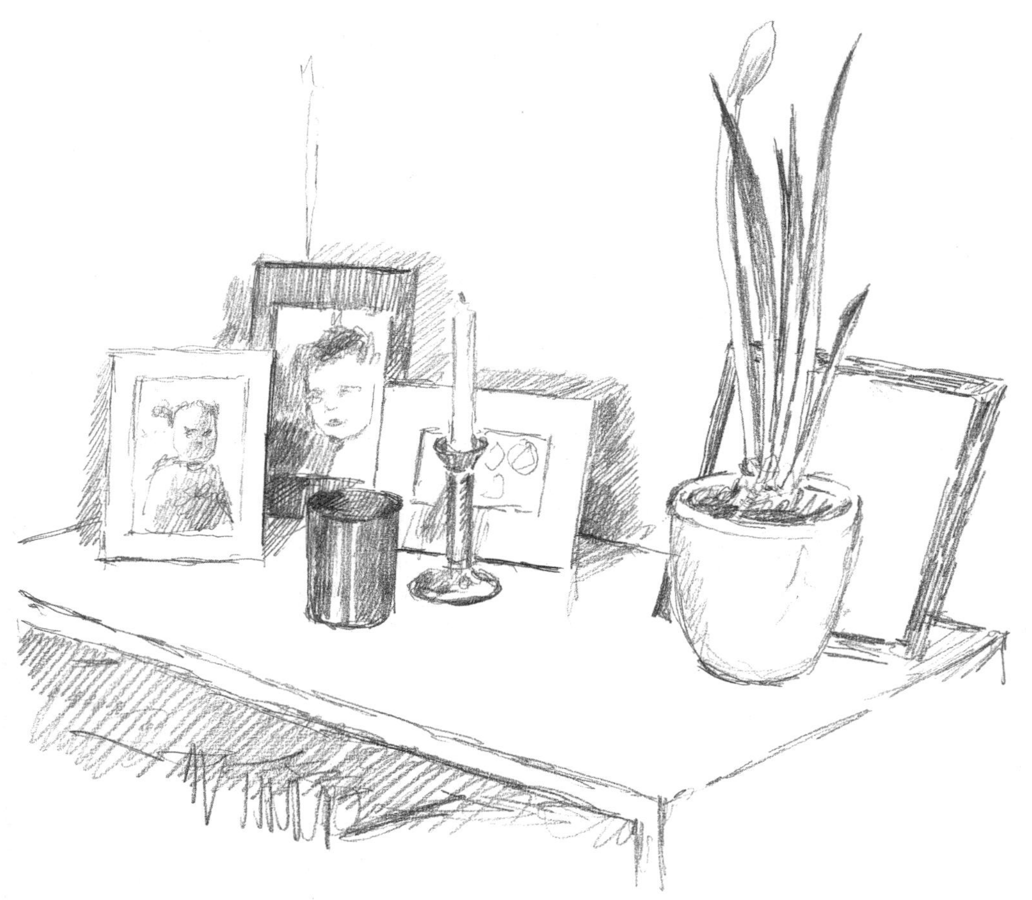

When I walked into my house I noticed a group of family photographs, some pots and a candlestick on top of a bookshelf. This was a more careful arrangement but not quite what I was after.

I then started collecting objects together that I thought might make a good group. From the kitchen I took a pestle and mortar, and from the top of the dresser a large jug.

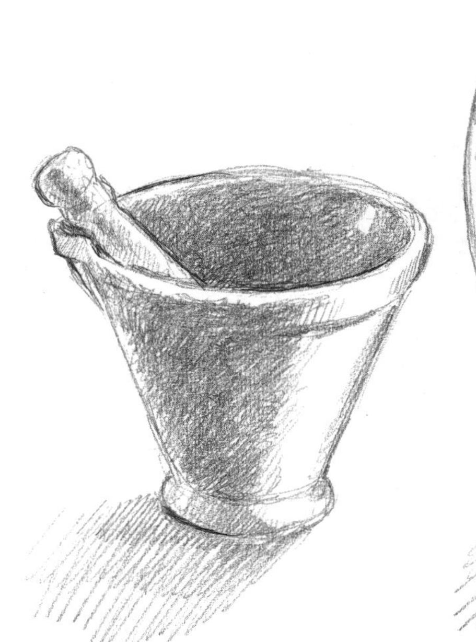

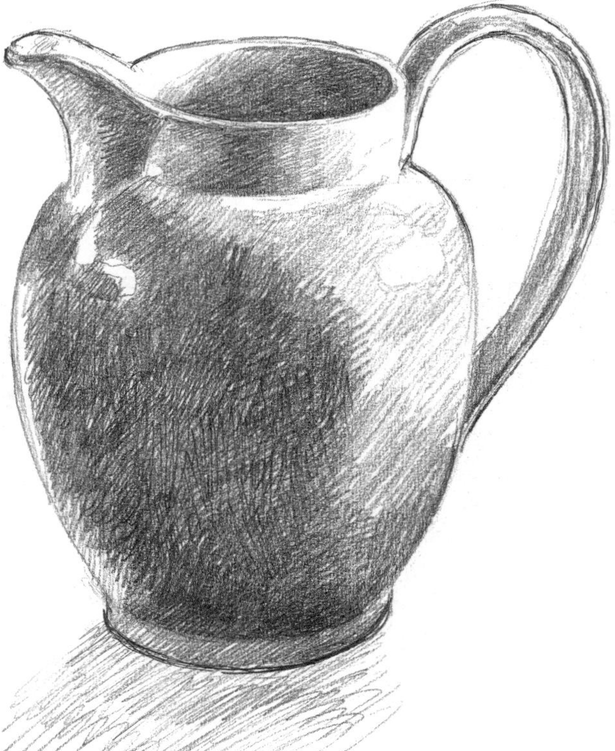

Preliminary Drawings

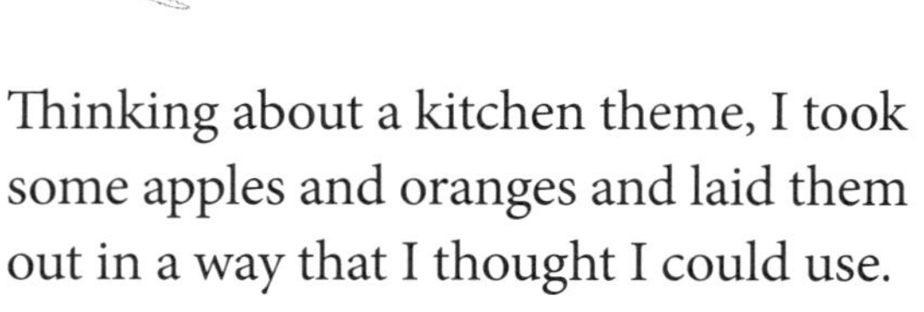

Thinking about a kitchen theme, I took some apples and oranges and laid them out in a way that I thought I could use. The theme seemed to be developing.

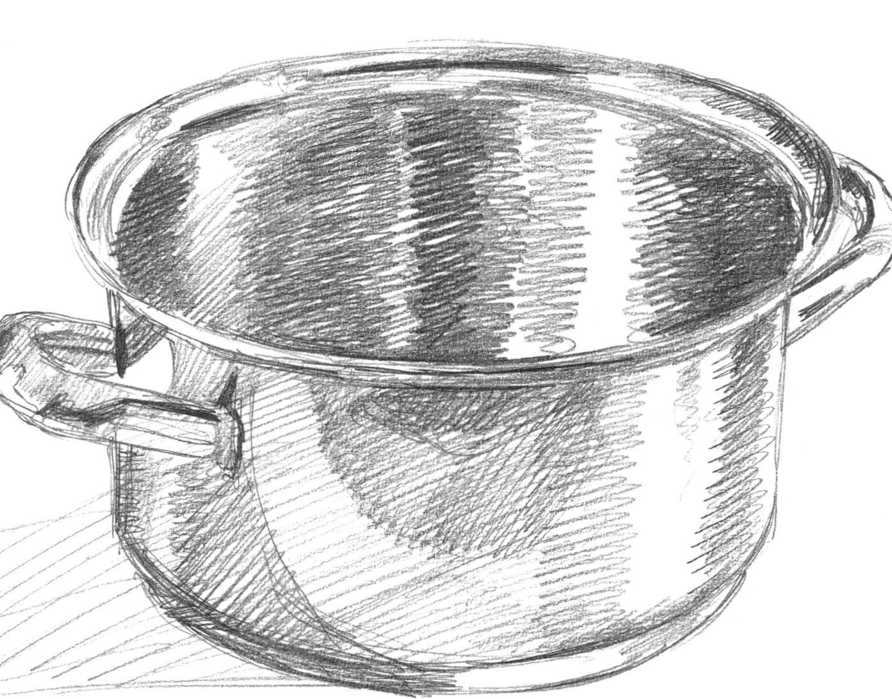

Next, to keep the idea going, I drew a large saucepan and then a couple of wine glasses. All this preparation is very useful for working up a good still-life composition. It may take you several days, but it's worth it when you are drawing a major piece of work.

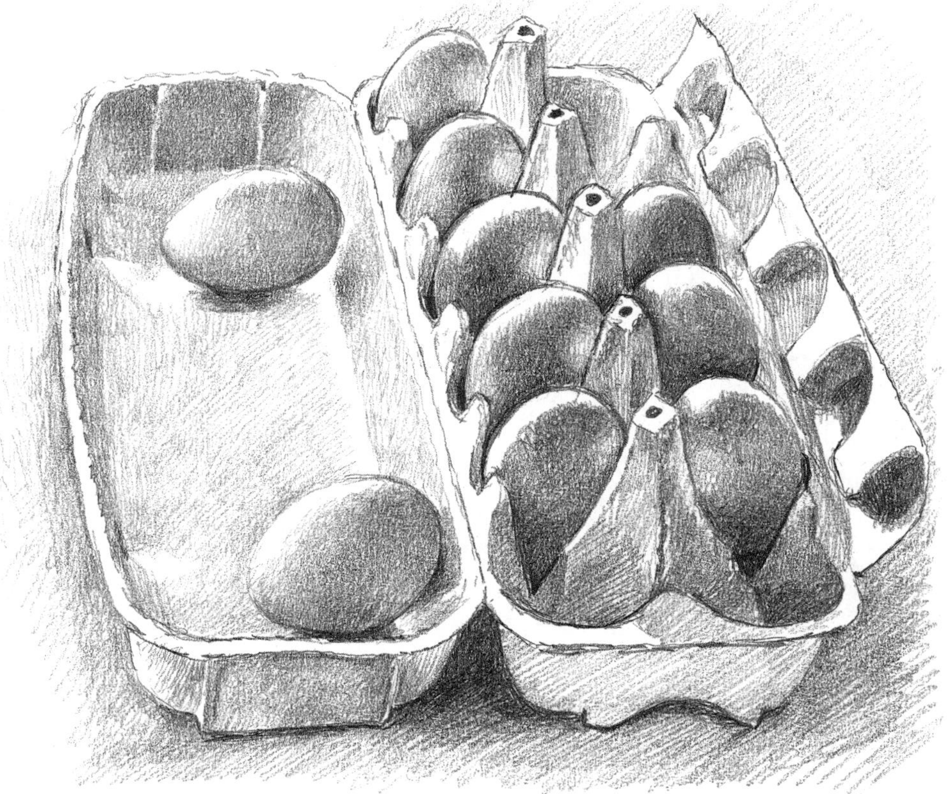

After that I added a bowl and, to bring in food again, a box of eggs from the fridge. My kitchen still life seemed to be falling into place.

I then put a napkin on the tabletop to add a different texture to the scene.

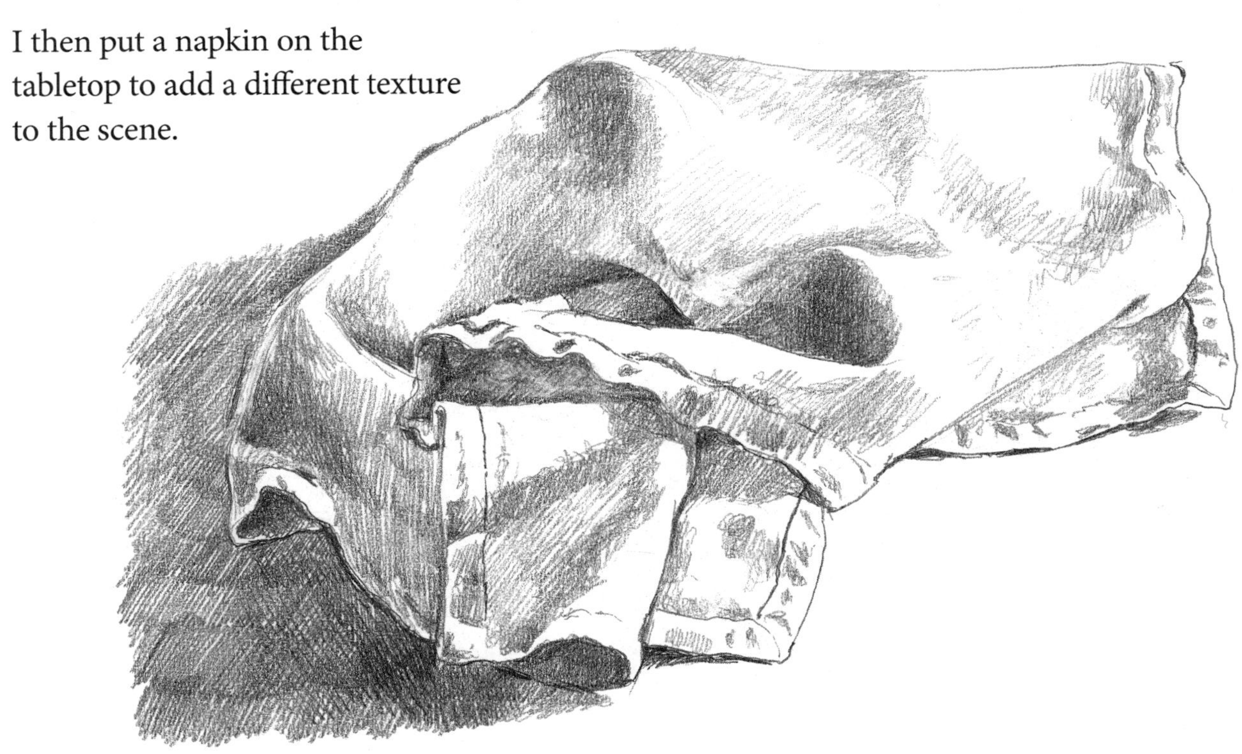

Choosing a Composition

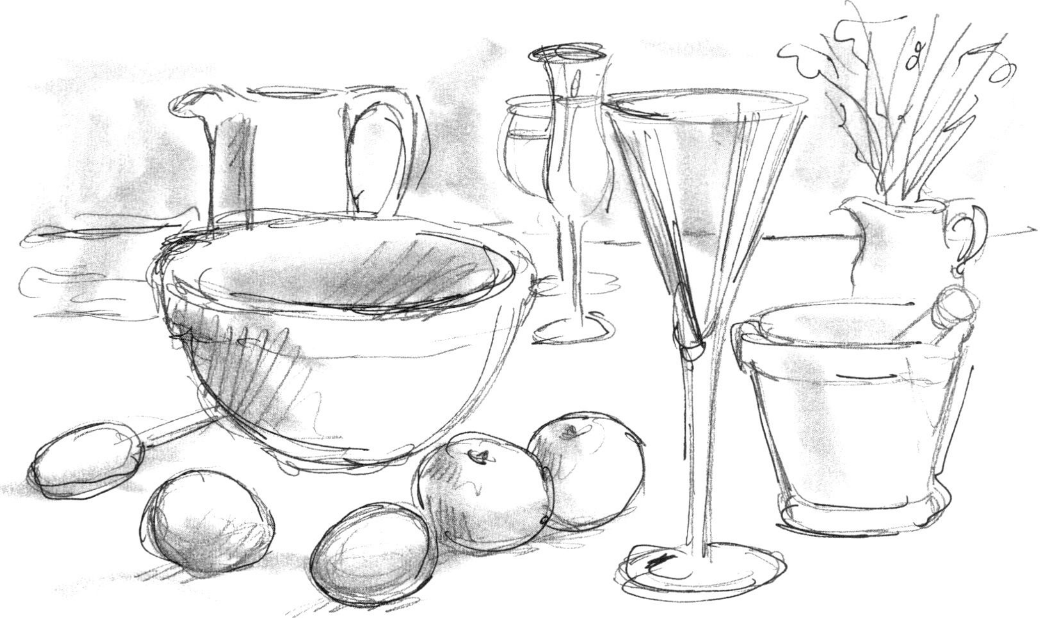

The next stage was to choose my composition pieces and try them out. I roughly scribbled out an arrangement of some of the objects I'd gathered.

Then I tried a much simpler one, but wasn't altogether convinced that it was interesting enough.

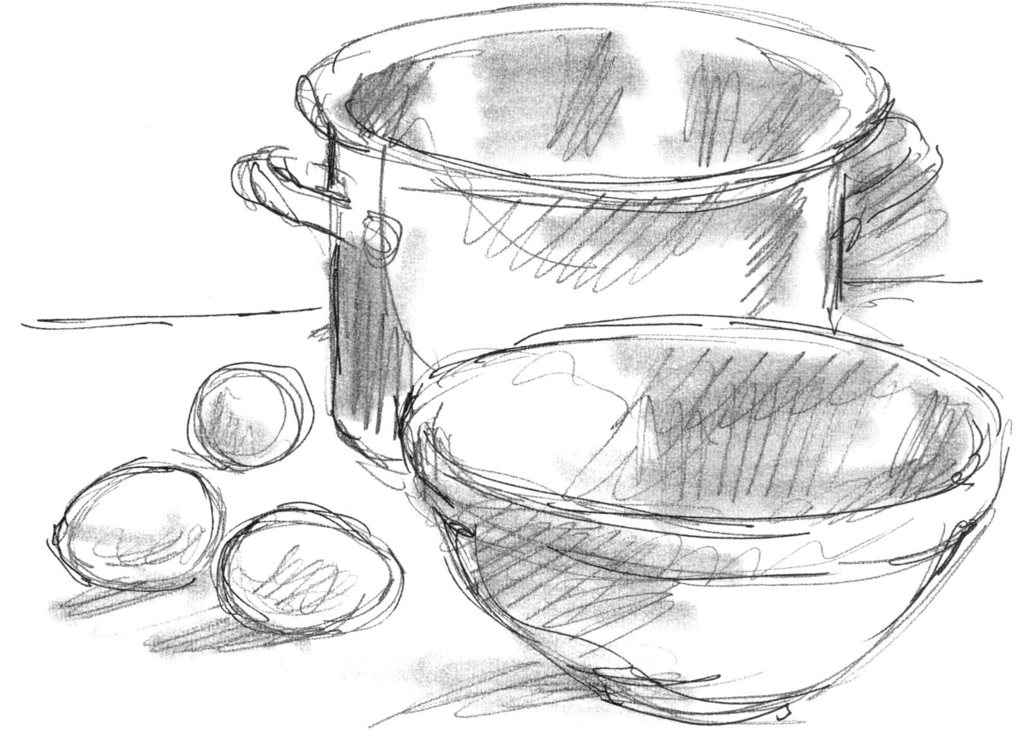

So I tried another arrangement but still felt it was not what I really wanted. This scribbling up of various compositions is never a waste of time, because it helps to clarify what you are really after.

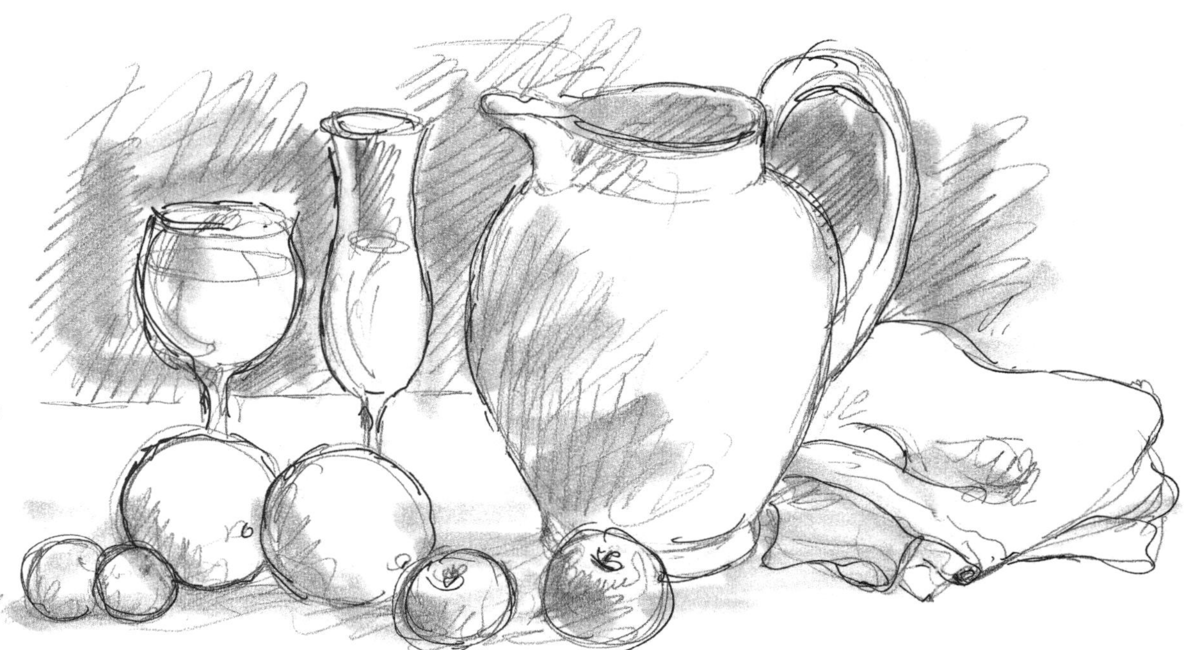

Finally I got something that started to look like the composition I wanted. All this preparatory work can be done long before you start to draw, but you do have to sit in the position that you think you will be drawing from when it comes to the real thing. Then you quickly start to see what it is that you find attractive.

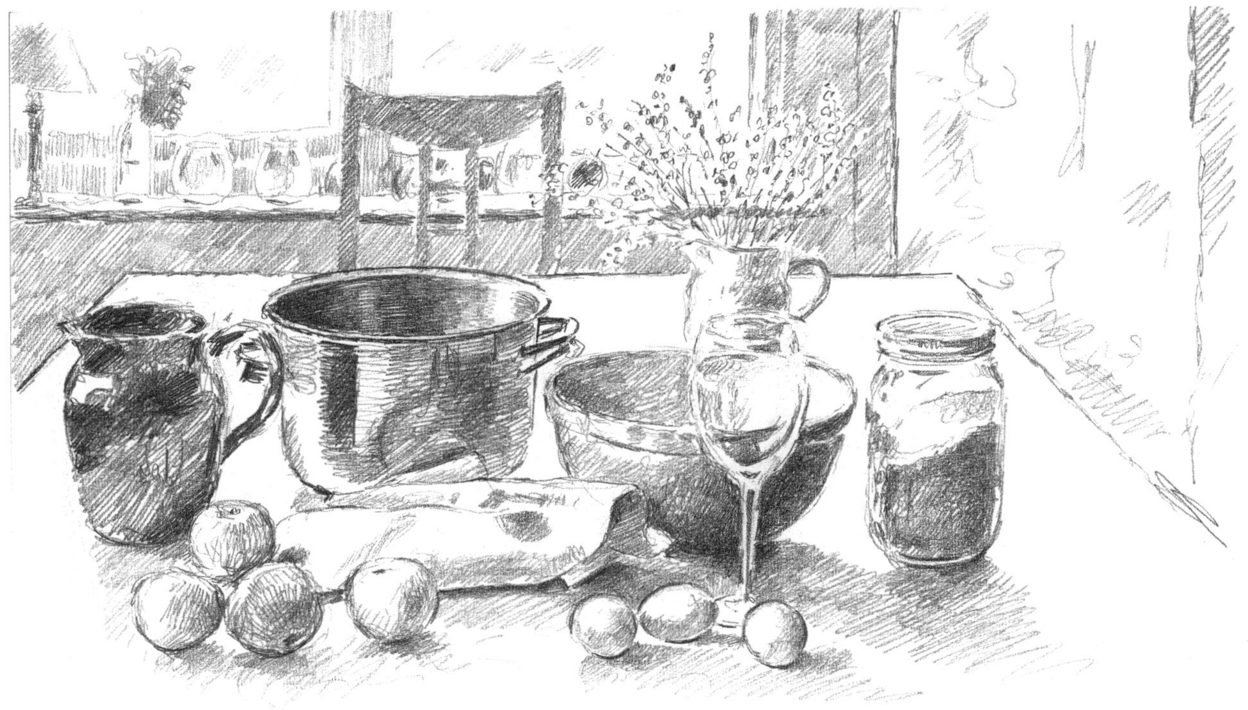

Final Composition

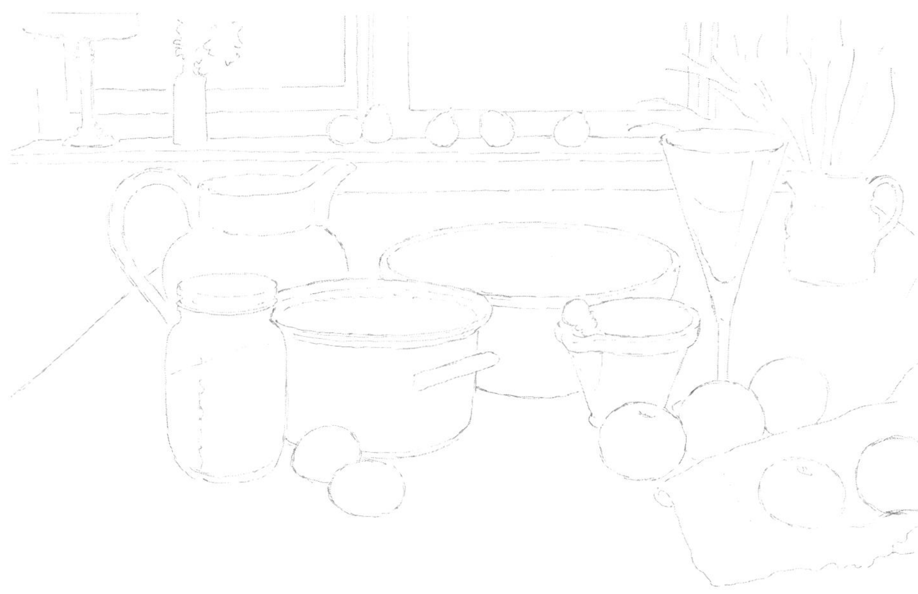

1. Now I had a good idea as to what the composition would look like. I carefully arranged all the objects I wanted to see in the drawing, sometimes swapping one object for a similar one in a different size or style. At this stage I drew up the whole composition in a light outline, correcting all the time in order to arrive at a clear cartoon drawing of the whole thing.

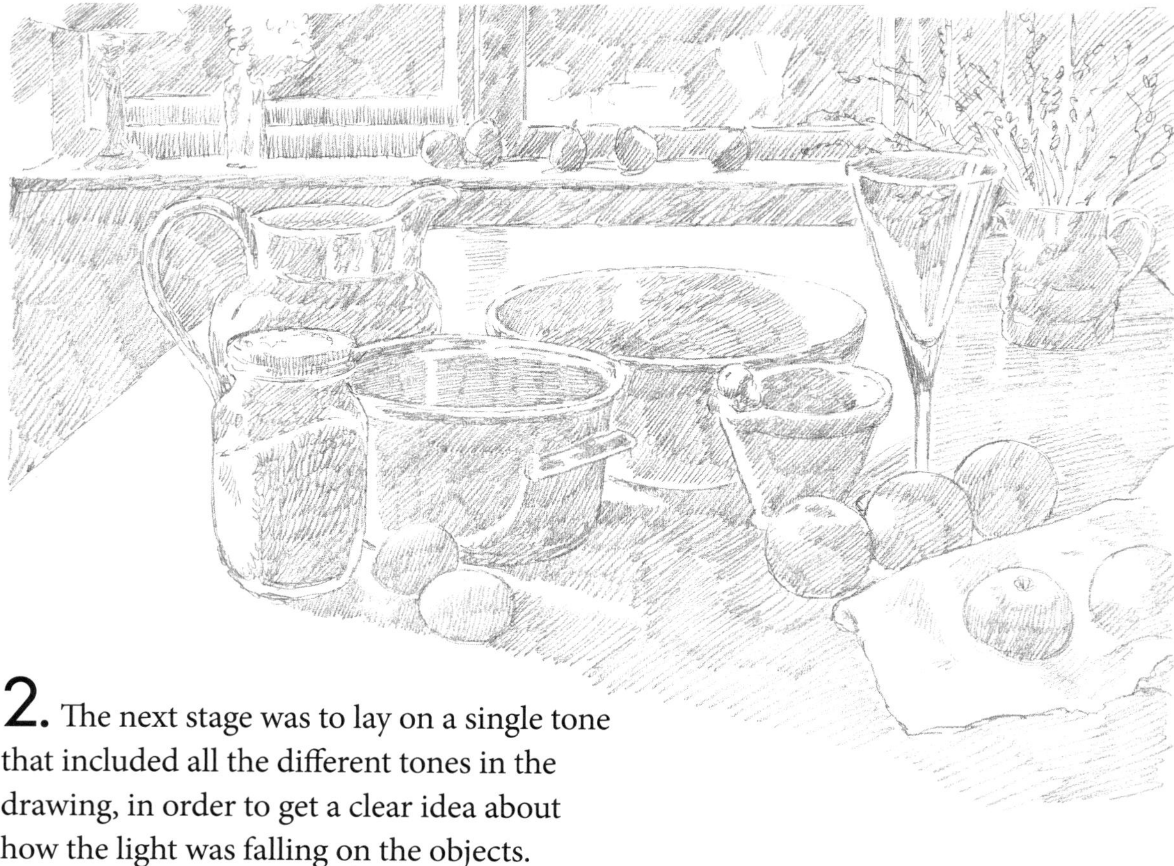

2. The next stage was to lay on a single tone that included all the different tones in the drawing, in order to get a clear idea about how the light was falling on the objects.

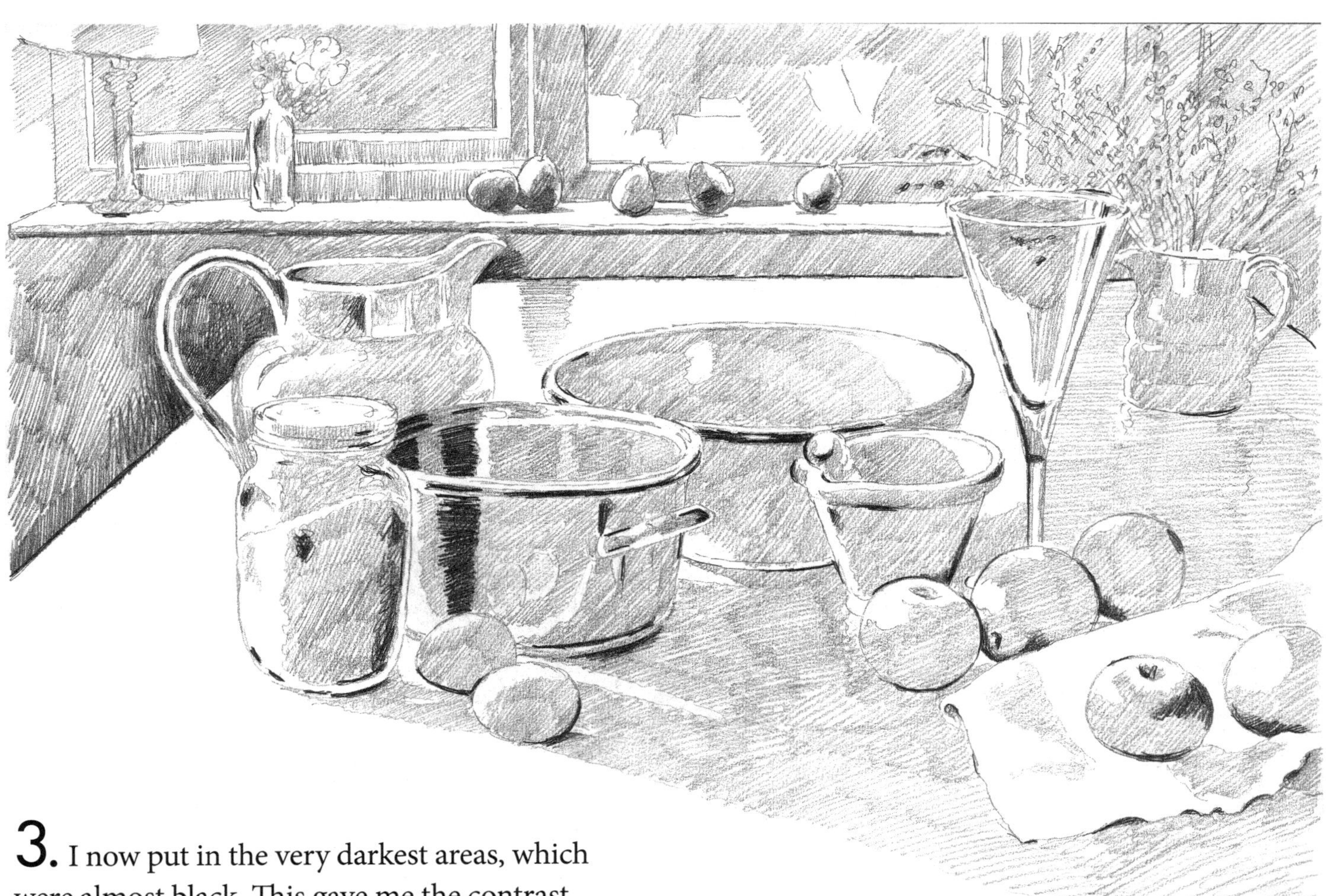

3. I now put in the very darkest areas, which were almost black. This gave me the contrast between the lightest and the darkest tones, and made it much easier to put in all the mid-tones. This can take some time but if it is done attentively it will really enhance the quality of the final picture.

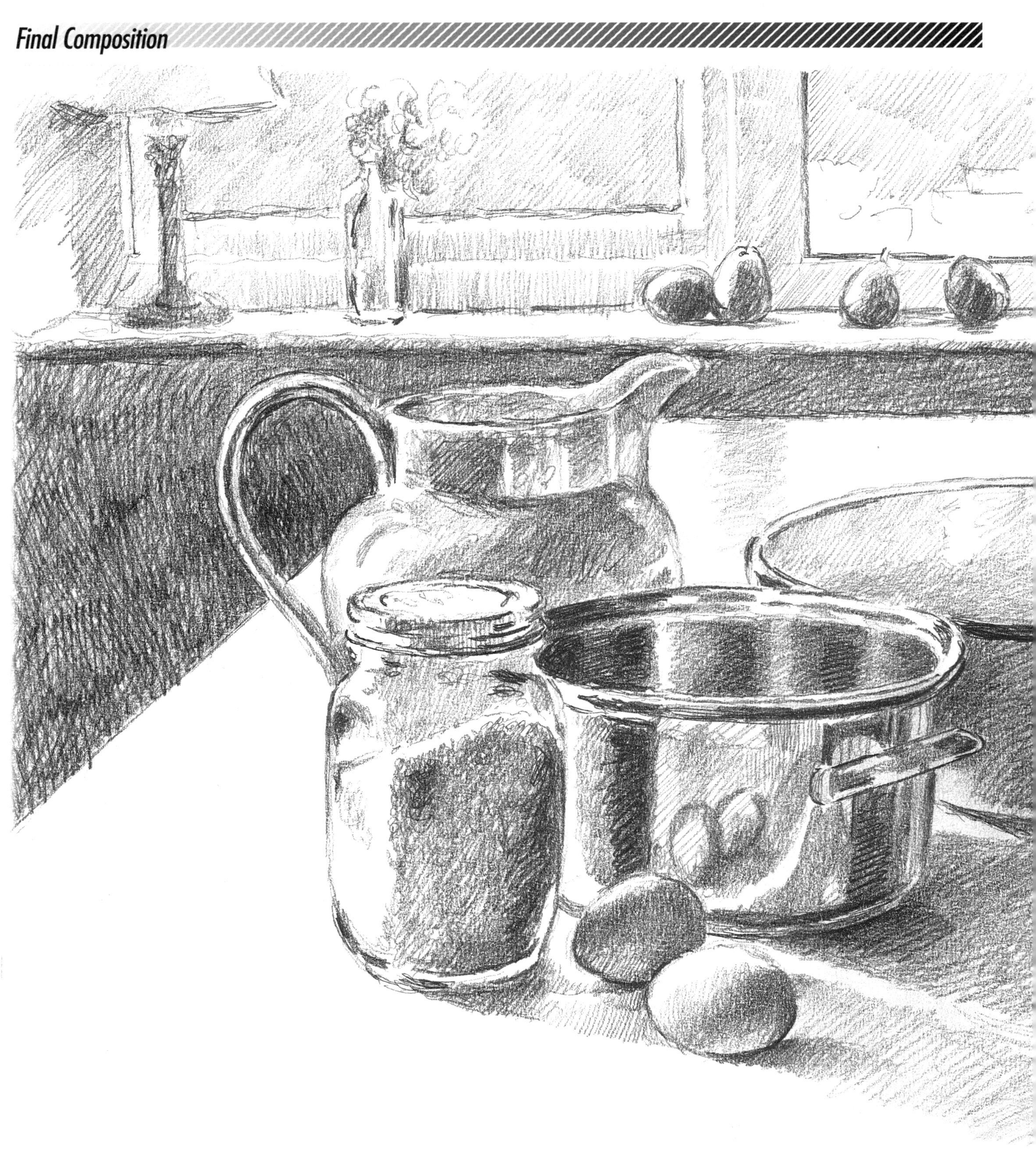

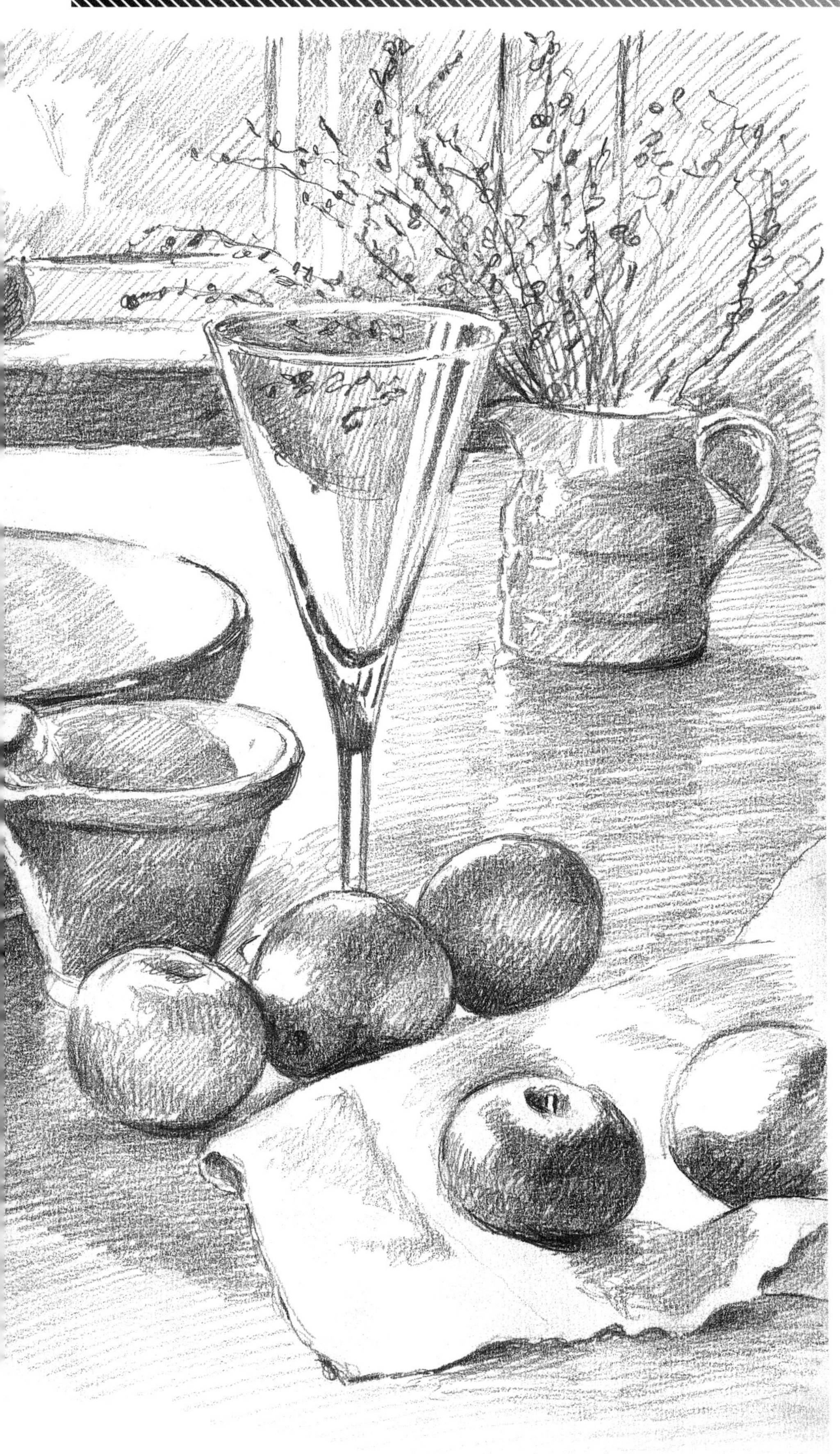

4. Finally, the tones between the darkest and lightest can be carefully graded to build a convincing three-dimensional effect, giving the appearance of light falling across the various objects and helping to indicate their texture and materiality.

Index

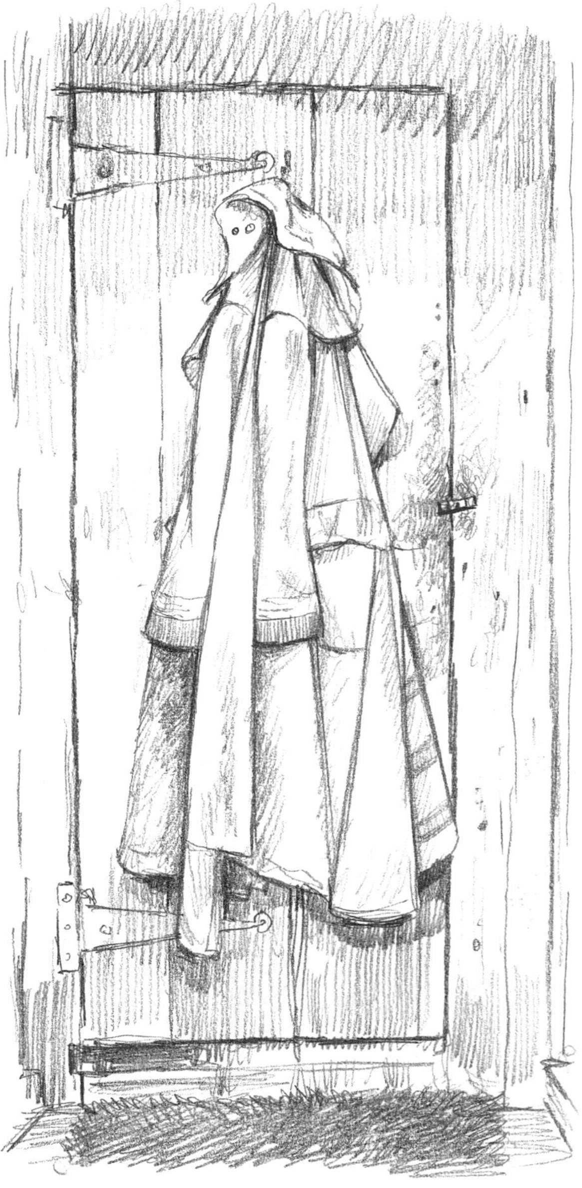

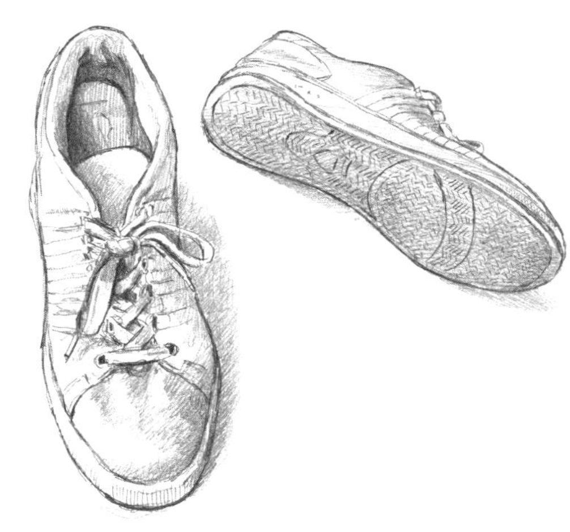